HARVEST OF HUMANITY

HARVEST
OF HUMANITY

JOHN T. SEAMANDS

VICTOR BOOKS ®
A DIVISION OF SCRIPTURE PRESS PUBLICATIONS INC.
USA CANADA ENGLAND

Unless otherwise noted, Scripture quotations are taken from the *Revised Standard Version of the Bible,* © 1946, 1952, 1971, 1973. Quotations marked NKJV are taken from *The New King James Version,* © 1979, 1980, 1982, Thomas Nelson, Inc., Publishers. Quotations marked KJV are from the *King James Version.*

Recommended Dewey Decimal Classification: 266
Suggested Subject Heading: MISSIONS

Library of Congress Catalog Card Number: 87-62485
ISBN: 0-89693-428-4

CONTENTS

PREFACE

In March 1986, I was in Pasadena, California, participating in dialogue with mission professors from Fuller School of World Mission, the E. Stanley Jones School of World Mission and Evangelism at Asbury Theological Seminary, Biola University, and Columbia Bible College. Under the leadership of Dr. Donald McGavran and Dr. Alan Tippett, we were discussing current issues and common problems. In one of the sessions, Dr. Tippett made the remark that "there is an urgent need for educating both pastors and lay people in the church as to what missions is all about in this day and age." He went on to explain how most church members today have a concept of Christian missions that was relevant in the nineteenth century, or even in the early part of this twentieth century, but is out of tune with the situation in 1986.

When I heard these words, something resonated within my heart and mind. I knew from personal experience that what Dr. Tippett said is true. For the past twenty-five years I have spent numerous weekends participating in church missions conferences all across the country. I have been in scores of churches and have met a large number of pastors and thousands of lay people. I found many who were genuinely interested in the missionary enterprise and gave generously to its cause but who did not have the faintest idea about the central objective of the Christian mission, the situation under which missionaries operate these days, the forces arrayed against the church, problems to be overcome, and new doors of opportunity that challenge us. This is tragic, for mission, the supreme task of the church, requires proper understanding for intelligent participation.

Missionaries are partly to blame for this situation. For when they speak to congregations in the home church, they tend to describe the dire physical and spiritual needs of people and to narrate all the success stories of their work. They are afraid to talk about disappointments and problems for fear that church members will be turned off to missions. "You see, those who give to missions want to know if their money has brought any results." There is truth in this statement, and certainly missionaries don't need to major on hardships and difficulties. But at the same time, supporters should understand some of the struggles that missionaries go through in order to be able to sympathize with them and to pray for them more intelligently.

So when I heard Dr. Tippett's comment, I decided then and there to do something about the situation. After all, for twenty-five years I have been telling prospective missionaries what missions is all about; why not tell the people back home—not so much from an academic but rather a practical standpoint? While the lecturer was still speaking, I jotted down several chapter titles as an outline, and when I got back home I started writing. The result is this book.

I have written all the material with the home church in mind. A deliberate attempt has been made to avoid technical jargon and to be as simple as possible. I have sought to describe:

—all the major mission issues that are being debated these days;

—the environmental forces that affect the world mission;

—the new movements that are shaping mission philosophy and strategy;

—and the unique doors that God has set before us.

It is my hope that this publication will serve as a study book for church groups, that it will be read carefully and discussed fully, and that it will bring information as well as inspiration. If the material leads the reader to a new understanding of the Christian mission, a more meaningful ministry of intercession, and more enthusiastic support for world evangelization, then the author will feel that his efforts have not been in vain.

PART ONE

BIBLICAL FOUNDATIONS—What Do the Scriptures Say?

The Christian mission is not a human enterprise, but a divine movement, originating in the very heart of God. It is not new, but as old as history itself. Ever since the creation of mankind, God has been reaching out to a fallen and sinful race. His method has been to use people to reach people. This fact is revealed in the Old Testament, where God through Abraham called out a people, Israel, to be His channel of blessing to the nations of the earth. It is seen in the New Testament, where Christ through His disciples called out a new people, His church, to be His instrument of redemption and service to the whole world. As part of the church today, our calling is still the same—to fulfill God's mission to all humankind. The church by its very nature is missionary at heart.

ONE

THE NATURE AND MISSION OF THE CHURCH

During World War II a story was going around about a German soldier who was wounded at the front. He was ordered to go to the military hospital for treatment. When he arrived at the large and imposing building, he saw two main doors, one marked "For those slightly wounded" and the other, "For those seriously wounded." He entered through the first door and found himself going down a long hall at the end of which were two more doors, one marked "For officers" and the other, "For non-officers." He entered through the latter and found himself going down another long hall at the end of which were two more doors, one marked "For Party members" and the other, "For non-Party members." He took the second door, but when he opened it, he found himself out on the street.

When the soldier returned home, his mother asked him, "Son, how did you get along at the hospital?"

"Well, Mother," he replied, "to tell the truth, the people there didn't do anything for me, but you just ought to see the tremendous organization they have!"

Is this a picture of the American church today? A lot of organization—many wheels turning, much busyness. But are we really doing business for the Lord? Are we bringing spiritual health and strength to those who are sick at heart and wounded in spirit?

This leads us to the main question: what is the nature and

13

mission of the Church? To most people, the church is the building down on the corner, where a group of people meet for an hour on Sunday morning, sing a few hymns, listen to a lecture, and then go home for lunch. We need a new concept of the church in scriptural terms if the church is to be what it ought to be.

What Is the Church?*

The church is an *organism,* not just an *organization.* It is a living fellowship where the Spirit of God is present and working, not just a club where members pay dues and attend meetings.

Several years ago there was an interesting program on the radio that broadcast a variety of sounds amplified several times above their normal volume. One of the sounds was that of a precision watch, claimed by the announcer to be "the world's most perfect timepiece." The watch ticked away: *click-clack, click-clack, click-clack.* Later in the program, the announcer said, "Now we want you to listen to the heartbeat of the world champion mile runner, Bob Mathias. There was the steady throb: *lub-dub, lub-dub, lub-dub.*

Here we have a wonderful illustration of the difference between an organization and an organism. The watch is a mechanism consisting of many parts, put together by man to tell the time of day. The heart is an organism, created by God to sustain life in the human body. The church of Jesus Christ is not a click-clack, a man-made organization, but a lub-dub, a Spirit-created organism that throbs with life and imparts life. Of course there will be organization in the church, but this will be only a means to an end, and not an end in itself or a substitute for life and mission.

Again, the church is an *instrument* of Christ, not just an *institution.* In the New Testament the church is spoken of as "the body of Christ," that is, His point of contact with the world, His workshop in the world.

At the close of World War II, a number of American soldiers were going through a heavily bombed town in

*From here to the end of this chapter is taken from a small, self-published volume entitled *Around the World for Christ.*

western Germany. Amidst the ruins of a church they found pieces of white marble that had been a statue of Christ. From sheer curiosity they gathered the pieces and fitted them back together, all but the hands, for they were nowhere to be found. The GI's debated among themselves whether to place the statue back on its pedestal. Without the hands, they realized, the statue had lost its beauty. Finally, they decided to restore the statue and write this inscription at the base: "He has no hands but yours."

How true! Christ has no hands but ours. The only way He can minister to the sick and downtrodden is through our hands. He has no feet but ours. The only way He can walk into the ghetto of our poverty-stricken slums or walk into the villages of India and Africa is through our feet. He has no lips but ours. The only way He can speak a word of comfort or tell of the Heavenly Father's love is through our lips. We, as members of Christ's body, are the instruments of His work in the world today. We are the agents of His mission.

What Is the Mission of the Church?

Bishop Azariah of India was once addressing a large company of Christian workers, and he told of the conversion of a Hindu to the Christian faith. The Hindu inquirer first read the Gospels and was fascinated by the teaching and miracles, the death and resurrection of our Lord. He said to himself, *I must follow this Man and become His disciple. There is none other like Him!* Then the Hindu seeker read on into the Book of the Acts of the Apostles. He was greatly impressed with the life and ministry of the early Christians. It seemed to him that they were carrying on in the flesh where Jesus left off at the end of His ministry. He said to himself, *I must not only follow Christ, I must also belong to the Christian church, for it seems to be carrying on the work that Christ came to do.* Bishop Azariah then said to his congregation, "Do the churches realize today that they exist to carry on the work that Jesus came to do?" A very pertinent question indeed!

What is the work that Jesus came to do? He Himself made this very clear during His public ministry. He said, "The Son of man is come to seek and to save that which was lost" (Luke 19:10, kjv). "The Son of man came not to be ministered unto, but to minister, and to give His life a ransom for many" (Mark 10:45, KJV). Jesus came to serve, to seek, and to save. This means that the mission of the church is to serve others, to seek and rescue the lost, and to give itself for the salvation of others.

Too long we have thought of the church in static terms of worship, of self-preservation. This is indeed part of the church's function: to minister to its own members, to inspire, to comfort, to instruct. The worship aspect, the coming together in fellowship, is important. We can't do without it. No one can live the Christian life in isolation. Everyone needs the spiritual help of the group. But to stop here is to become selfish and ingrown. What would we think of a football team that stayed in the huddle all the time? The huddle is important for the players to get their cues and to encourage one another. But the huddle is not an end in itself. The players huddle in order to advance toward a touchdown. Any church that spends all its time huddling in worship without ever getting into the game of evangelism and social action is not worthy to be called a "church" in the New Testament sense of the term. The whole point of Jesus' Parable of the Good Samaritan is just this: it is not enough to worship in the temple; we must help needy people along the highway.

We must, therefore, conceive of the church in functional terms of movement, ministry, and sharing. The institutional aspect is a means to the end. The real point of it all is ministering in the midst of humanity. The church is both the gathering and the scattering of the people of God—gathering for worship, learning, and spiritual growth; scattering for witness and service, permeating society at every level. The redeemed community is the redeeming community. Mission is thus built-in. An automobile needs to stop for gas and servicing occasionally, but it was not made for the service station. It was made for the highway. A ship is safe in the harbor, but it was not made for the harbor. It was made for the high seas, to split the waves on the way to some destination. The church exists, not to be a closed fellowship, but to be an instrument of redemption to the total needs of humanity.

Someone has compared the church to a fishing fleet. From the mother ship the individual boats are launched daily to carry each fisherman to his task. To the mother ship each boat returns regularly, bringing its prizes, and the fisherman replenishes and renews his strength. The church must keep a proper balance between worship and witness, between gathering for spiritual growth and dispersing for service.

Where Is the Mission of the Church?

Jesus made it clear that this ministry of service and redemption is directed to the whole world. He commanded His disciples, "Go therefore and make disciples of all nations. . . . Go into all the world and preach the gospel to the whole creation" (Matt. 28:19 and Mark 16:15). He reminded them that "repentance and forgiveness of sins should be preached in His name to all nations, beginning from Jerusalem," and that they should be His witnesses "in Jerusalem and in all Judea and Samaria and to the end of the earth" (Luke 24:47 and Acts 1:8). The church has a worldwide mission, and every disciple of Christ must have a world-encompassing vision.

Some years ago in one of our mission boarding schools in India, the youngsters were putting on an evening of entertainment with music, recitation, and drama. A young lad of twelve years of age was asked to give the opening prayer. In keeping with his age, he prayed a simple yet sincere prayer. He asked the Lord to bless those who took part and those who watched. Then he suddenly remembered that in a few days annual examinations would begin, so he prayed, "Dear Lord, in a few days we'll be having examinations; please help me to pass." But then he realized that he had prayed only for himself, so he quickly added, "Lord, help everyone in my class to pass the exam." After a slight pause he went on, "Lord, help everyone in the whole school to pass." Another pause, then, "Lord, help everyone in all the schools to pass the exam." Then it seemed that his vision and faith were mounting, and he burst out, "Lord, let the whole world pass!"

As disciples of Christ, we need a vision and concern that goes beyond ourselves, our own congregation, our own nation—one that encompasses all nations and peoples, so that our constant prayer shall be, "Lord, let the whole world be redeemed!"

Each local congregation should formulate a program that ministers—in accordance with its total resources—to the needs of the whole world. Of course, it is impossible for any one church, with its limited resources, to supply total physical and spiritual needs of all people everywhere. But it can, in some small measure, minister to some of the people in various parts of the world. Then if each congregation does its part, the whole world can be served. A simple yet practical plan is suggested in the diagram.

Each local church has a responsibility to its own membership. Its own spiritual life must be renewed constantly. Jesus said to Peter, "Feed My sheep" (John 21:17). The members of the congregation must be spiritually nurtured, encouraged, guided, and trained until they all reach spiritual maturity. This is accomplished through the regular ministry of the church, the pastor acting as shepherd. The Sunday worship service, Sunday School, midweek prayer service all should be geared to the purpose of spiritual nurture and instruction.

Further help can be gained through annual preaching missions, special services, weekend retreats, prayer cells, and study groups. A constant attempt must be made to transform those members who are nominally Christian into genuine disciples of Jesus Christ. Those who are halfhearted must be transformed into totally committed disciples. Those who are born of the Spirit must become filled with the Spirit. The fruit and gifts of the Spirit must be evident in the lives of all.

This inner renewal, however, is not to be an end in itself. Its primary purpose is to enable the congregation to minister redemptively outside of its own membership. While the congregation is ministering to its own needs, it must look beyond itself and minister to the needs of the community. This can be accomplished by a well-planned program of evangelism and social action.

Jesus not only told Peter that he was to be a shepherd of the sheep, but also that he was to be a fisher of men. The local church, therefore, must serve "by hook and by crook"—the fisherman's hook and the shepherd's crook. This work of evangelism can be carried on by the personal witness of the members in their various vocations—in the office, factory, classroom, playground, and store. It can be implemented by house-to-house visitation, as members call on their neighbors and in an informal setting share their faith in Jesus Christ with those who never darken the door of the church. At times special preaching missions can be held on a citywide basis in some neutral territory, such as a school gymnasium or a stadium. The more the members share their faith with others, the stronger and more meaningful their faith will become.

Evangelism must be coupled with social action. The two cannot be separated, like the two wings of a bird or the two rails of the railway track. Dr. Stanley Jones said that "evangelism without social action is like a soul without a body; social action without evangelism is like a body without a soul. One is a ghost and the other is a corpse. We don't want either. We must keep evangelism and social action together. Then we have a living organism."

Jesus made it clear that He is deeply concerned about the poor and the sick and the captive. He said that when we minister to such people, we minister to Him, and when we fail to minister to such people, we fail to minister to Him. He warned that one of the bases of our judgment shall be our attitude and action (or lack of action) to those who are in need (Matt. 25:31-46).

The poor, the sick, the despised are found in every community. The local congregation should keep its eyes open to the manifold needs all about and should share its resources in personnel and funds to help meet those needs. Professional persons can make a contribution by donating some of their time using their skills for the welfare of those who would normally not be able to afford such services. If there are social service centers already in operation in town, congregations can cooperate to help strengthen and enlarge their ministry. Such projects usually require adequate facilities with a large budget, so that it may be better for several churches to cooperate rather than for each individual congregation to work alone.

Besides involvement in community affairs, each local congregation should have a share in "home missions" in some part of the nation. This can best be accomplished by working through regular denominational or ecumenical agencies. Gifts of money can be made; gifts of service can be offered by members during vacation time. Mission projects in the inner city, the ghetto, Appalachia, and Indian reservations are examples of possibilities in the area of home missions.

Finally, local congregations must lift up their eyes and look out upon the fields across the seas. Christianity is a begin-at-home religion, but not a stay-at-home religion. Jesus said we are to begin at Jerusalem (hometown), then proceed to Judea and Samaria (adjoining areas), and never stop until we have reached the ends of the earth. A practical plan of involvement in foreign missions would be for each church to accept a project in each of the major cultural (or geographic) areas of the world: Europe, Latin America, the Islamic world (Middle East), Africa, Southeast Asia, and the Far East. If a small congregation feels that this is entirely unrealistic and going beyond the possibilities of its limited resources, it may vary the plan by each year accepting a missionary project in a different area of the world—one year in Africa, the next year in Latin America, the following year in Asia, and so on. The principle is that each congregation must have the world in its vision and on its heart. Christ is interested in the whole world; so His followers must be.

In this ever-widening circle of involvement—beginning with inner renewal and proceeding on to community service, home missions, and foreign missions—each local congregation can consider itself a center of Christian ministry from which blessing and healing emanate to the entire world. This is the ideal toward which all congregations should strive.

J. Allan Ranck, in his book *Education for Mission* (Friendship Press), writes:

> The mission of the church is like a pool of water into which thousands of pebbles are dropped. Concentric circles move out from the place where each pebble breaks the surface, and the circles mingle with one another until the whole pool is agitated. There is not just one center from which the circles expand; there are centers everywhere. . . . Wherever there is a church, or for that matter, an individual Christian, the mission begins. From the center it moves out until it involves the church and the Christian in the evangelization of the whole world. (p. 4)

Who Is Responsible for the Mission of the Church?

Is it the sole responsibility of the preacher? Most church members seem to believe so. Or at least, they act as if this were true. Many a congregation could be compared to a football team that sends the coach out on the field to play the game all by himself while the "players" sit on the bench as spectators. Many church members feel that the pastor is paid to do the preaching, praying, visiting, witnessing, and serving. They don't feel personally involved in the mission of the church. It is time that the spectators, who are sitting on the pews, get on the team and into the game.

I heard a story—most likely apocryphal—of a football fan who attended the games regularly and rooted for his home team. During one important game, when the championship was at stake, a player of the opposing team intercepted the ball and was headed for a certain touchdown. The fan got all excited, rushed out onto the field, tackled the runner, and brought him down. The crowd went wild and a riot almost ensued. Referees finally declared a touchdown for the team who had possession of the ball.

"A foolish thing for the fan to do," you say, and I agree. But at the same time I admire the spirit of the man. He could no longer remain a spectator on the sidelines; he had to get into the game. How I wish some of our church people, sitting on the sidelines for years, would get so excited about the mission of the church that they could no longer remain as silent spectators!

It is not the task of the pastor to work *for* his people. He must work *with* them. He must be a playing coach. He will train the team and at times call the play, but he himself is to be in the game, and so ought every member of his congregation.

One of the most effective methods of evangelism developed in recent years is that called Evangelism in Depth. It was initiated by R. Kenneth Strachan, late General Director of the Latin American Mission, and has been used with considerable success in several Central and South American republics. The church in many of these lands has been completely revitalized, and thousands of people outside the church have been brought to faith in Jesus Christ.

The inspiration for the Evangelism in Depth program came to Strachan when he began to ponder the reasons that certain movements or groups were growing throughout the world, such as Communists, Mormons, Jehovah's Witnesses, and the Pentecostals. Here were four movements, one anti-Christian, two pseudo-Christian, and the fourth Christian but not in the conventional pattern, all increasing in numbers and influence. What was the secret of their advance? Was it their doctrine? That could not be, because each was preaching a different message. Was it their method, their organization, their emphasis? The answer did not seem to lie with any of these. Finally Strachan came to recognize that, in spite of their many differences in doctrine, organization, emphasis, and practice, they were alike in only one thing—and that one thing was the secret of their success.

What they had in common was this: their success in mobilizing their total constituency in continuous evangelistic action. And so Strachan came to the conviction that the secret of expansion was to be found in this thesis: the expansion of any movement is in direct proportion to its success in mobilizing its total membership in continuous propagation of its beliefs. Evangelism in Depth is founded on "total mobilization of the church for total outreach."

But this is New Testament Christianity! This is what God always intended for His church!

We must realize that the church of Jesus Christ is a living organism with the Holy Spirit at the center of its life, that the church exists for a redemptive mission to the entire world, and thand that each one is involved in this mission. Then alone will the church as the body of Christ fulfill its God-given purpose in our world.

TWO

THE ROOTS OF
THE CHRISTIAN MISSION

A few years ago, Alex Haley, an American black, wrote a book entitled *Roots,* in which he traced his ancestry back several generations to a family in an African village. The story was later portrayed in a TV series and was seen by millions of viewers across the country. Since then there has been new interest among Americans to "trace their roots" and rediscover their heritage. People want to know where they came from.

The church of Jesus Christ today needs to rediscover its roots and the heritage of its mission. Did its mission originate in the mind of man or in the heart of God?

For the roots of the Christian mission we have to go back to the Scriptures themselves. But how far back do we go? Just to the Gospels in the New Testament, or all the way back to Genesis in the Old Testament? Do we seek out a proof text, an isolated command? Or do we trace the hand of God throughout the Scriptures?

Somebody asked the Duke of Wellington, the famous English general who defeated Napoleon, whether a Christian should be interested in missions or not. The Duke responded with another question: "What has your commander in chief said about the matter?"

The man answered, "Christ has commanded us to go into all the world and preach the Gospel to every creature."

"Well, then," said the Duke, "that settles the question. Now it is up to you to obey."

We would naturally expect a military officer to argue in such a manner, for when a command is given in the army, it is to be obeyed without question. But does the Christian mission rest solely on a single command given by the Lord Jesus Christ? Or does it rest on the message and tone of the entire Bible?

Actually, the missionary mandate was given long before the Great Commission was announced by the resurrected Christ. It was first given by God in the Book of Genesis, when He chose Abraham to become the father of a new nation. God said to Abraham:

> Get out of your country, from your kindred and from your father's house, to a land that I will show you. I will make you a great nation; I will bless you and make your name great; and you shall be a blessing. I will bless those who bless you, and I will curse him who curses you; and in you all the families of the earth shall be blessed. (Gen. 12:1-3, NKJV)

Notice what God said to Abram, "I will bless you . . . and you shall be a blessing. . . . I will bless you . . . and in you all the families of the earth will be blessed." God didn't choose Abram and the nation of Israel just so they might be His pets or favorites. He chose them for a missionary purpose—that through them the light of salvation might shine upon all peoples of the earth. Privilege involved responsibility. The tragedy is that the people of Israel failed to live up to their calling.

The significance of the Genesis missionary mandate is seen in the fact that both Jesus and Paul referred to it in their teachings. After His resurrection Jesus met two disciples on the way to Emmaus. Shortly afterward, He appeared to the eleven disciples in Jerusalem. He found them all despondent and without hope. Then He chided them for not perceiving the necessity of His death and the missionary mandate that was revealed in the Old Testament, in the Law of Moses, the Prophets, and the Psalms. Luke, the historian, writes in his Gospel:

And He opened their understanding, that they might comprehend the Scriptures. Then He said to them, "Thus it is written, and thus it was necessary for the Christ to suffer and to rise from the dead the third day, and that repentance and remission of sins should be preached in His name to all nations, beginning in Jerusalem. (Luke 24:45-47, NKJV)

Paul, writing to the church at Galatia, also reminded his readers of the missionary mandate given to their forefathers.

And the Scripture, foreseeing that God would justify the nations by faith, preached the Gospel to Abraham beforehand, saying, "In you all the nations shall be blessed." (Gal. 3:8, NKJV)

Thus, the missionary mandate is far older than the Great Commission given by our Lord in the Gospels. It goes way back to the Book of Genesis, to the beginning of the Jewish nation. It is rooted in the Old Testament and reiterated in the New Testament. The Christian mission, therefore, does not rest on one solitary command or two or three isolated verses; it is grounded in the entire body of Scripture. The Bible is a missionary book. The Old Testament portrays God's plan of redemption for all people. The Gospels in the New Testament record the coming of God's great Missionary to the world. The Book of Acts describes the activities of the early Christian missionaries. The Pauline Epistles are letters written by a missionary to the churches he had founded. The Book of Revelation describes the final consummation of God's missionary activities.

Now we are in a position to examine in detail the full biblical basis of the Christian mission. Why should we as Christians be interested and involved in the world mission of the church of Jesus Christ?

Mission Is Inherent in the Nature of God

God is a missionary God. The Word tells us that God is love. Love is the very essence, the very fiber of His being. All of His actions spring from this basic characteristic.

Love always takes the initiative. It is outgoing; it is self-giving. It is concerned for others; it gives itself to others. Thus, "God so loved the world that He gave His only begotten Son that whoever believes in Him should not perish but have everlasting life" (John 3:16). "Herein is love, not that we loved God, but that He loved us, and sent His Son to be the propitiation for our sins" (1 John 4:10, KJV). "Hereby perceive we the love of God, because He laid down His life for us" (1 John 3:16, KJV).

Love is all-inclusive, all-embracing. It is no respecter of persons; it recognizes no distinctions. Thus, God so loved the *world*—not white people only, not just Americans or Methodists—but the world, humanity as a whole. God's great purpose from the beginning was the redemption of the entire human race. It is His will that all should be redeemed, that none should perish. The Gospel was intended for, and is adapted to, every race and clime and condition of humanity.

The Bible is simply the record of God's missionary activities. It is the story of His sovereign redeeming acts having become decisively and finally manifest in Jesus Christ. It traces the activity of God from the beginning before all beginnings. Our love, our communion with Him is involved in the very creation. It is for this fellowship that we are made. The history of God's dealings with the nation of Israel is the history of His concern for the world and His love for people, which kept Him reaching out His hand to them. The covenant, Exodus, the prophets' ministry, the remnant's return from exile—all these were evidence of His presence and signs of His loving, saving intent.

In the life and death of Jesus we see most unmistakably, and most compellingly, the missionary character of God. As David Livingstone once said, "God had only one Son, and He became a missionary." In Jesus we see the loving concern of the Father for needy people. We see Him healing the blind and the leper, ministering to the poor and the downtrodden, speaking the word of forgiveness to the sinful outcast. He identified Himself with the sin and suffering of humanity. He was called "a man of sorrows and acquainted with grief" (Isa. 53:3).

In Jesus, we see the sacrificial love of the Father. He not

only came to us and became one of us, but He also gave Himself for us. In Jesus on the cross, God laid His love alongside the sin of the world. He gave Himself so that we might be reconciled to Him and live in that fellowship for which we were made. No difficulty or obstacle that the world contrived could stop Him. His was a love that did not even balk at rejection. There on the cross He is seen as the loving God who penetrated into every pocket of sin and loneliness and futility. He put an end to our frantic and futile search for Him and His will. He made the whole process obsolete by coming into human life, showing us Himself and His intent.

The Holy Spirit is the originator and director of the Christian mission. He is the chief Personality in the Book of Acts, not Peter or Paul or Barnabas. It was when the disciples were filled with the Holy Spirit that the church was born and the missionary movement was inaugurated. The Holy Spirit empowered the early Christians for witnessing and preaching and guided them as to what they should say before the elders and magistrates. It was the Holy Spirit who scattered the disciples so they would spread the Gospel to all Judea and Samaria. He is the One who directed Peter to go to the household of Cornelius, the Roman centurion, and who directed Philip to go to Gaza, where he met the Ethiopian official. The Holy Spirit called Paul and Barnabas out of Antioch and sent them into Asia Minor and across to Europe.

Thus, mission finds its origin in the very nature of God, revealed to us so clearly in the record of the Old Testament, in the life and death of His Son, and in the ministry of His Spirit. The Triune God is a missionary God. Can we be anything else?

Mission Is Inherent in the Christian Faith

At least two major points make the Christian faith missionary by nature. First, its exclusive claims. The Bible doesn't picture God as *a* god, one among many. He is the *only* God. "There is no God but one" (1 Cor. 8:4). "There is one God, and there is one mediator between God and men, the Man Christ Jesus" (1 Tim. 2:5). Further, the Word doesn't picture Christ as *a* Saviour. He is the *only* Saviour. "There is salvation in no one else, for there is no other name under heaven given among men by which we must be saved" (Acts 4:12). Since there is only one God and one Saviour, then He must be presented to the world. Since there is only one Gospel that can offer eternal life, it must be proclaimed to the world.

Again, the Christian view of humanity makes the Christian faith missionary. The Word pictures all persons as lost, condemned by God because of their sin. "All have sinned and fall short of the glory of God" (Rom. 3:23). Sin has alienated everyone from God, has corrupted human nature, and has brought condemnation and death. No one is free from it; no one can deliver himself from it. If the biblical view of people is false, then there is no need for any missionary. If people after all are basically good; if sin is not so tragic after all; or if we can plead that ignorance relieves people from guilt and condemnation, then missions are not imperative. But if the biblical picture of people is true, then missions are an urgent necessity.

The very nature of the Gospel makes it missionary. The Gospel is good news. It is the good news that God has not left us in our sins, but has loved us so much that He gave His Son to live and die and be raised again that we might be redeemed from all sin. It is the good news that God is *not against us* because of our sin, but He is *for us* against our sin. News must be told; it cannot be kept secret. It is the very characteristic of news that it must be proclaimed. That is what they do with the daily news of the world. That is what we must do with the eternal news of God.

One day the medical profession will discover a cure for cancer. When they do, it will be good news. And they will be obligated because of the very nature of the case to share this news with the world. The Christian Gospel is good news, news of God's sure remedy for the dread disease of sin. By the very nature of the case it must be shared with the world. Thus, the missionary enterprise is not an afterthought, an addition to the Gospel. It *is* Christianity.

Christianity's destiny is to be universal. Its favorite word is *all*. It appears more than seventy times in Romans alone. *Whosoever, any, all*—these are words that appear over and over again in the New Testament.

Mission Is Inherent in Christian Discipleship

If God is missionary in nature, and the Christian faith is missionary in character, can the Christian be anything else? The Christian life is primarily a relationship to God the Father and to Christ the Saviour. The Christian is one who has been "born of God" and has become a "child of God." He is one who has entered "into Christ" and become a "new creature" by His grace. As a child he partakes of the divine nature and acquires the spirit and outlook of the Heavenly Father. Since love is one of the chief characteristics of the Father, it now becomes one of the chief characteristics of His spiritual offspring. The Father loves the world and is concerned for all people; so are His sons and daughters. The Father gives Himself in loving service and sacrifice for the redemption of the world; so do His sons and daughters.

The truth is brought out so clearly in the Parable of the Prodigal Son that Jesus told. The elder brother in the story stayed at home and worked in his father's field, but he was out of tune with his father's spirit. He was not a good son because he was not a good brother. When the younger son came home, the father welcomed him with open arms and rejoiced in his return. But the elder brother was jealous and angry, complained to his father, and would not join in the festivities. And this was one of the main points of the parable. Jesus was saying to the Pharisees who stood nearby: "You are more interested in lost sheep and lost coins than you are in lost people. If a sheep gets lost, you'll scour the hillside until you find it. If a coin gets lost, you'll sweep the whole house to find it. But if a boy or girl gets lost, you do nothing about it. In fact, you grumble and criticize when someone comes home." What Jesus was saying was that if we are true sons and daughters, we will be interested in what the Father is interested in, namely, finding lost people.

I shall never forget a Bible study on this same parable given by a missionary doctor in India several years ago. At the end he said: "I can imagine that not long after the younger son came home from the far country, he must have gone to his father and said: 'Dad, I want to go back to the far country and I would like to have your permission.' The father probably said, 'Son, don't mention it. You left home once and broke your mother's heart and mine. Please don't go!' " Then the doctor went on to explain: "The son smiled and said, 'Dad, the first time I left home it was to satisfy my own selfish desires. But this time it is different. When I was out in the far country, I saw many sons and daughters away from home. I want to go back and tell them that if they return home, Father will be waiting to receive them with joy.' "

That is the sign of a good son—concern for the lost.

It is time we make it clear that the Christian mission arises directly and solely from our relationship to God. After all is said and done, missions are established and missionaries go out because the missionary impulse is born with the new person in Christ, because to be a Christian is to be missionary in heart and mind. When we know the Lord, we must make our Lord known to others.

The missionary motive, therefore, is not an obligation to do something, but a response to Someone. It is not a dutiful reaction to a particular command, but a loving response to the Person of Christ. It is not a deduction of logic, but a reflex of faith. Why do Christians witness at home and abroad? Because they are bound to Christ, who is at work everywhere. Thus *all* Christians are missionary in spirit. It is not a matter of duty, but of disposition. Mission is in the Christians' blood. The only kind of Christian there is, is missionary. A nonmissionary Christian is a contradiction in terms—like wooden iron or a round square. We *all* are caught up in Christ's struggle; we *all* respond to a missionary God; we *all* witness to a witnessing Lord.

Now for some the mission may be accomplished at home in a parish or on a campus. Others will be called by equipment, preparation, interest, and the challenge of the church to those farther fields that we designate with the word "missions" in a technical, professional sense. But all are being Christian in their own areas; that is, they are missionaries where they are. And only insofar as they are, are they being Christian.

Mission Is Inherent in the Life of the Church

What this whole analysis of the Christian response does is to turn the whole Christian membership into a missionary reservoir, because it is a missionary fellowship. If God is a missionary God, then His institution, the church, will be a missionary institution. If Christ, the great divine missionary to the world, is the head of the church, then the church as His body will be a missionary body. If each individual Christian is a missionary by virtue of his relationship to his Lord, then the church, as a fellowship of Christian disciples, will be a missionary community.

The church does not simply *have* mission, but it *is* mission. It does not just have a missionary *department,* but a missionary *disposition.* The church, insofar as it is a church, is missionary. It is the witnessing fellowship of those who have been witnessed to, the reaching body of those who have been reached, the forgiving fellowship of the forgiven, the redemptive society of the redeemed, the outgoing family of those who have been gathered in.

Mission, therefore, is primary, not secondary; fundamental, not optional. Mission constitutes the primary work of the church, the work for which it was commissioned by our Lord. The missionary movement is not simply a desirable thing for the church to carry forward, but it is its chief and most important undertaking. It is the reason for the existence of the church, and should be made a controlling purpose in the life of the members.

The church has one mission: to make Jesus Christ known to the world and to accomplish the mission that Jesus Himself came to achieve. Jesus realized that He had been sent to the world to do the work of His Father. His life and death were devoted to it; His resurrection vindicated it. To His disciples and His church, Christ said, "As the Father has sent Me, even so I send you" (John 20:21). As God made Himself known in Jesus Christ, so Christ sends His church into the world to make Himself known. God was in Christ reconciling the world to Himself, and now He entrusts to us the message of reconciliation (2 Cor. 5:19). The church exists only for the purpose of Christ's mission.

The vitality of the church depends on its being missionary. As Emil Brunner said, "The Church exists by mission, as fire exists by burning." This is the circulation of its lifeblood, which would lose its vital power if it never flowed forth to the extremities, but curdled at the heart. A nonmissionary church will suffer atrophy; a missionary church will possess abounding spiritual life.

A local church fulfills its mission in part in its own community. It proclaims the Word of God. It teaches. It leads people into fellowship with God and offers fellowship with other Christians. It leads people into God's presence through Word and sacrament. It speaks on community issues and ministers to community needs.

When the church extends these ministries to other communities, close at hand or far away, then it affirms the New Testament teaching that the mission is to reach from "Jerusalem and Judea to Samaria and the uttermost parts of the earth." This reaching out we identify as the missionary work of the church. Christian missions exist to tell the good news of the Gospel. Their aim is to establish the church in every place,place, working in partnership with people who confess Jesus Christ as their Saviour and Lord. They seek to extend the reign of God in individuals and society across the world.

THREE

THE SIGNIFICANCE OF THE GREAT COMMISSION

Although the Great Commission is not the primary basis for Christian mission, it does provide much impetus for the missionary enterprise. It is significant because it constitutes Christ's last command to His disciples and brings into focus the entire missionary theme and objective that runs from Genesis to Acts. It is the climax of all that has gone before.

The impact of the Great Commission was undoubtedly one major spiritual factor that inaugurated the modern Protestant missionary movement under William Carey late in the eighteenth century. For the first 250 years of Protestant Reformation, Christians were not seriously engaged in world mission. There were many reasons for this lack of missionary concern and involvement, but one of them was the fact that Christians believed that the Great Commission was given by Christ solely to His immediate disciples. It was William Carey who finally convinced the church that the commission was intended for all Christians of all times. It was this conviction that gave impetus to the greatest missionary movement in Christian church history.

The Great Commission is recorded in each of the four Gospels and in the Book of Acts. That fivefold command is common in its central thought and aim, yet each of the evangelists gives his own special emphasis through the inspiration of the Holy Spirit. Matthew emphasizes Christ's authority and presence and discipling of the nations. Mark accentuates the universality of the commission and responsibility of the hearers. Luke stresses content of the message and power to proclaim it. John features the spiritual qualifications and demands.

Let us now take a close look at each one of the Great Commission statements and see what it has to say to us.

The Great Commission in Matthew

Now the eleven disciples went to Galilee, to the mountain to which Jesus had directed them. And when they saw Him they worshiped Him; but some doubted. And Jesus came and said to them, "All authority in heaven and on earth has been given to Me. Go therefore and make disciples of all nations, baptizing them in the name of the Father and of the Son and of the Holy Spirit, teaching them to observe all that I have commanded you; and lo, I am with you always, to the close of the age." (Matt. 28:16-20)

This is a general commission. Christ spoke as King in the consciousness of His resurrection glory and universal dominion. He first established His claim to deity (v. 18), and then issued His requirement that divine honors should be paid to Him the world over (vv. 19-20). We see here the *power* of the King ("all authority has been given to Me"), the *purpose* of the King ("make disciples of all nations"), the *program* of the King ("make disciples . . . baptizing . . . teaching"), and the *presence* of the King ("I am with you always").

Matthew declares the primary objective of the missionary enterprise: to make disciples. This is the key verb of the entire passage of Scripture. The going, baptizing, and teaching all center on the task of making disciples. A disciple is more than just a believer. A disciple is a lifelong follower of Christ, committed to the Lord's will and subject to the disciplines of the Christian way.

The emphasis in Matthew's Gospel is on crossing *ethnic frontiers.* We are to disciple "all nations." The word *nation* here does not refer to sovereign political states, such as the 221 nations affiliated with the United Nations. *Nation* refers to people groups—races, tribes, clans, castes, classes, etc.

Within a single political unit there may be scores, even hundreds of different ethnic, linguistic, social, and cultural groupings of people. Our task is not merely to evangelize in every country, but to make disciples from among all the peoples of the earth. The Great Commission forbids any form of racism, provincialism, or nationalism. Christ desires to build His church with people of all races, languages, and cultures.

It is to be noted that *teaching* is to be added to *preaching,* which means that systematic instruction is to be given wherever disciples are made. It doesn't take much knowledge about the Christian faith for a person to become a believer, but to become a mature disciple takes continued study of the Scriptures and practice in everyday life. This means evangelism in *depth* as well as in *width.*

Matthew's version of the Great Commission may be epitomized under two small yet important words—*go* and *lo.* "Go and make disciples . . . lo, I am with you always." Christ sealed His command with a promise. First He commanded His disciples to go, and then He promised that He would go along with them, through the indwelling presence of the Holy Spirit. Christ never asks us to go anywhere He is not willing to go Himself. In fact, when we go forth in His name, we usually find He has gone on ahead of us, preparing the way for our coming. That is what happened when the Spirit ordered Philip the evangelist to leave Samaria and go down to Gaza (Acts 8:26-40). When Philip met the Ethiopian official he found him reading the fifty-third chapter of Isaiah, which pointed to the suffering Messiah. What better preparation could Philip have had in order to preach Jesus as the crucified Saviour?

We must take note at this point that the *lo* is always linked up with the *go.* The promise follows the command. Many of us gladly claim the promise of Christ's presence, but we are reluctant to obey the command to go forth and make disciples. We have no right to quote the promise unless we are willing to assume our responsibility. Christ's presence is not given to us for personal enjoyment, but as an endowment for service.

Finally, notice the fourfold use of the word *all* in the Great

Commission as recorded by Matthew. "*All* authority has been given to Me . . . make disciples of *all* nations . . . teaching them to observe *all* things . . . lo, I am with you *always.*" This is an enterprise based on the full authority of Christ, involving the whole body of His teachings, relating to all peoples of the world, and intended for all times.

The Great Commission in Mark

And He said to them, "Go into all the world and preach the Gospel to the whole creation. He who believes and is baptized will be saved; but he who does not believe will be condemned." (Mark 16:15-16)

This statement of the Great Commission is grand, simple, and comprehensive. The emphasis is on *preaching,* proclaiming the good news in Christ. We are to preach *the Gospel.* John Stott points out that the Gospel of the New Testament consists of the Gospel *events*—Christ died and rose again; the Gospel *affirmations*—Christ is both Saviour and Lord; the Gospel *demands*—repent and believe; and the Gospel *promises*—you shall receive forgiveness of sins and the gift of the Holy Spirit (*Christian Mission in the Modern World,* InterVarsity Press, pp. 44–54). Our preaching is based on the Person of Christ, not on a system of ethics or a set of rules.

Whereas Matthew emphasizes *ethnic* frontiers ("all nations"), Mark emphasizes *geographical* frontiers ("all the world . . . the whole creation"). We are to proclaim the Gospel in all continents, every country, every island. We are to cross the street, cross the mountains, and cross the seas until everyone has heard the good news of Christ.

Our preaching is for a verdict—that people might believe in Christ and be saved. Thus, evangelism consists of *presence* (going among the people), *proclamation* (preaching the Gospel), and *persuasion* (seeking a decision).

Mark not only accentuates the responsibility of Christ's followers (to go and preach the Gospel), but the responsibility of the hearers as well (to repent in faith). Salvation by faith is the keynote here.

As in Matthew, there is a faint reference to the fellowship of the church in the word *baptized.* The new disciples are not to be left in isolation, but are to be incorporated into the body of Christ, for mutual support and corporate worship.

The Great Commission in Luke

Then He opened their minds to understand the scriptures, and said to them, "Thus it is written, that the Christ should suffer and on the third day rise from the dead, and that repentance and forgiveness of sins should be preached in His name to all nations, beginning from Jerusalem. You are witnesses of these things. And behold, I send the promise of My Father upon you; but stay in the city, until you are clothed with power from on high." (Luke 24:45-49)

You shall receive power when the Holy Spirit has come upon you; and you shall be My witnesses in Jerusalem and in all Judea and Samaria to the end of the earth. (Acts 1:8)

The Great Commission recorded by Luke emphasizes the primary calling of the missionary. The missionary is to be essentially a witness for Christ. Jesus said, "You are witnesses of these things . . . you shall be witnesses." Thus, Jesus enunciated the fundamental truth that the disciples would be effective messengers to needy persons only in the measure that they had a personal knowledge of God and witnessed to facts that they knew. Their witness is based on the testimony of the biblical record and their own personal experience.

It is significant that Jesus did not say, "You shall witness to Me," but "you shall *be* witnesses." True witness is rooted in *being,* not just in speaking; in *character,* not merely in communication. We must first witness with our *lives* and then with our *lips.* So we add a fourth ingredient to evangelism. Evangelism consists of *presence* (going), *proclamation* (preaching), *practice* (being), and *persuasion* (preaching for a verdict).

The word *witness* comes from the Greek word *martus,* from which we derive the English word *martyr.* This is suggestive, for the thought of martyrdom is at the heart of all true acts of witnessing. Testifying to Christ and salvation by grace alone means spiritual death to one's self and all natural conceptions of salvation. It may, at times, mean physical death at the hands of those who are hostile to the Saviour. It certainly implies the idea of self-giving.

Luke is the only one who emphasizes the *content* of the Christian message—"repentance and forgiveness of sins should be preached in His name." This message is founded on the death and resurrection of our Lord—"It is written that Christ should suffer and on the third day rise from the dead."

Note that repentance is added to the requirement of faith mentioned in Mark's Gospel. The two cannot be separated. Saving faith grows out of a true spirit of repentance, for only when people recognize their sins will they turn to the Saviour for forgiveness.

Whereas Matthew emphasizes *ethnic* frontiers, and Mark, *geographical* frontiers, Luke stresses both. In his Gospel he writes: "Repentance and forgiveness of sins should be preached in His name to *all nations* [ethnic frontiers], beginning from *Jerusalem* [geographical frontiers]." In the Book of Acts he writes: "You shall be My witnesses in Jerusalem and in all Judea and Samaria and to the end of the earth." Here we have the divine program of missions: we are to reach people of all races, languages, and cultures, and we are to begin where we are (in Jerusalem) and never pause until we reach the uttermost part of the earth. If we are not witnesses at home, in our own families and neighborhoods, then it is not likely that we will be witnesses in some far-off place. For it is not *crossing the seas,* but *seeing the cross,* that makes us missionaries.

Luke not only places emphasis on the content of the message and the central calling of the missionary, but also the power available to proclaim the message and to be effective witnesses for Christ. Jesus said to His disciples, "You shall receive power when the Holy Spirit has come upon you, and you shall be My witnesses." He also commanded them to "tarry in the city of Jerusalem until you are endued with power from on high." The Christian mission is a divine enterprise and requires divine resources for its fulfillment. As Dr. E. Stanley Jones used to say, "The human spirit fails unless the Holy Spirit fills." So we dare not go forth to preach until first we have tarried for the power.

Look at the difference in the lives and ministry of the disciples of Christ before and after Pentecost. Before the outpouring of the Holy Spirit in His fullness, the disciples often displayed moments of weakness. Sometimes there was uncertainty, or doubt, or carnal fear of people. This was especially true in the last days before Calvary. They forsook their Master and went into hiding. Peter shamefully denied his Lord. But after the experience of Pentecost, the disciples displayed a stronger faith, a new spirit of confidence and courage. They possessed a power beyond themselves to withstand persecution and temptation and to witness boldly to the resurrection of the Lord.

How the church today needs this supernatural power— power to reach out beyond the confines of brick and mortar, and to carry the spiritual offensive into the strongholds of society. The church needs power to break out of routine and formality and to perform exploits in the Master's name; power to call people to repentance and true righteousness; power to transform individuals and change society.

The church of our day has great buildings, but little boldness. It has numbers, but little nerve. It has comfort, but little courage. It has status, but lacks spirit. It has prestige, but little power.

The Great Commission in John

"As the Father has sent Me, even so I send you." And when He had said this, He breathed on them, and said to them, "Receive the Holy Spirit." (John 20:21-22)

John's version of the Great Commission is short but profound. He leads us into a deeper meaning of the whole missionary enterprise.

The other Gospel versions look *manward* in their perspective: "Make disciples of all nations," "preach the Gospel to every creature," and "be My witnesses in Jerusalem, Judea, Samaria, and to the end of the earth." The emphasis is on the people to be reached or evangelized. In John's Gospel, Christ looks *Godward* rather than manward, showing us that the

Great Commission had its origin in the very heart of God, and that its fulfillment depends on our relationship to Him. The Christian mission thus has a vertical as well as a horizontal dimension. There is first our vertical relationship to the Heavenly Father and then our horizontal responsibility to all our fellow men and women. If we are born of God and partake of His nature, then we will be concerned about His creation. If we are sons and daughters of God, then we will be servants to the people of the world.

Then again, John's version of the Great Commission makes the missionary enterprise Christ-centered in its nature. The key word in this verse is the word "as"—"*as* the Father has sent Me, so send I you." In the other Gospels, the emphasis is on *action:* Go make disciples, go preach the Gospel, baptize, and teach. Here the emphasis is on the *disposition* of the missionary, on character, rather than deeds. Like Father, like Son; like Christ, so His disciples. The same relationship that existed between Father and Son must now exist between Christ and His disciples—a relationship of love, faith, and obedience. The followers of Christ must go forth in the same spirit in which He came—a spirit of humility and self-renunciation (Phil. 2:5-8). They must go forth with the same attitude that motivated Christ—not to be served, but to serve (Mark 10:45). They must seek to engage themselves in the same mission that Christ came to fulfill—to seek and to save the lost. Christ's followers must share in His suffering, bear His cross, and have the print of the nails in their daily lives.

Again, in this Gospel there is a clear reference to the essential ministry of the Holy Spirit in the whole missionary enterprise. After Jesus gave His commission to the disciples, He breathed on them and said, "Receive the Holy Spirit." The infilling of the Holy Spirit is not only necessary to empower us for action, but also to purify our hearts and instill within us Christlike attitudes and motives. The Holy Spirit enables us to be what we should be in order for us to do what we should do.

Again look at the disciples of Christ before and after Pentecost. Before Pentecost they exhibited a spirit of pride; they argued who was the greatest among them. They displayed an attitude of selfishness; they sought for thrones on the right and left of Christ. They were angry at the Samaritans because of their lack of hospitality and wanted to call down fire from heaven to consume them. But after the experience of Pentecost, the disciples were completely changed. Instead of pride, there was now humility. They were no longer self-seeking, but self-giving, ready to be the servants of all. Instead of hating the people of Samaria, they preached the Gospel to them in love.

There is an intrinsic relationship between Pentecost and missions. Pentecost is the essential preparation for mission, and mission is the natural outcome of Pentecost. The presence of the Holy Spirit within us lifts the missionary motivation from mere obedience to an external command to compulsion of an inner drive.

Summary

We are now ready to make a synthesis of the fivefold statements of the Great Commission and see what is the total impact from all the Gospel writers.

The missionary enterprise involves the Trinity. God sent the Son; the Son sends us; the Holy Spirit goes with us. The mission of the church is God-inspired, Christ-centered, and Spirit-directed.

The missionary enterprise involves the world. *All* disciples of Christ are called to be partners in the great program; these disciples are instructed to go to *all* peoples and *all* lands. They are to start where they are (Jerusalem) and go to the end of the earth.

The missionary is a "sent one," sent to proclaim a message and to serve. The message is basically repentance and remission of sins. He is given power to proclaim this message. But the true missionary must not only have a message; he must be the living embodiment of that message and the incarnation of the truth he teaches. He stands as witness to the truth he possesses and proclaims it by his life as well as by his lips.

The program of missions involves evangelization—preaching; instruction—teaching; and assimilation—baptizing.

The Christian message is *universal* (for all nations and lands); *historical* (based on facts to which we witness); and *practical* (that we might believe and be saved).

PART TWO

CRUCIAL ISSUES—What Is the Truth of the Matter?

In recent years a movement has gained momentum in some Christian circles, leading us away from our biblical foundations. This has produced a division in our ranks. Some Christian leaders claim that the primary mission of the church is to proclaim the Gospel and establish the church of Jesus Christ in every land. Others claim it is to challenge evil social and political structures and establish justice and liberty throughout the world. There is a tendency for both sides to go to extremes. One group emphasizes evangelism, and the other, social action. We all need to get back to our biblical roots to find the answer.

THE NATURE OF THE CHRISTIAN MISSION

Having considered the strategic importance of mission throughout the Scriptures, let us now turn our attention to the nature and objective of this mission. In recent years, the mission of the church has been defined in two almost exclusive ways. They are commonly known as the *traditional* (or evangelical) view and the *ecumenical* view of mission. Some people believe that the chief business of the church is evangelism and church planting, while others contend that it is involvement in the sociopolitical issues of the day.

The Traditional (Evangelical) View

The traditional view equates mission with evangelism. The ultimate objective is to make Jesus Christ known to all people in all lands as the divine Saviour and Lord, to the end that they should become His disciples and be established in indigenous churches. The emphasis is on proclamation, conversion, and church planting. Establishing churches is not considered an end in itself, but a means to further evangelization. This means the national church will in turn evangelize its own people and establish additional congregations— the church will reproduce itself. What was once the object of evangelism now becomes the agent for further evangelism.

Those who have held this view have by no means neglected the social services. They have carried on excellent educa-

45

tional and medical work, but they considered these merely as springboards or aids to evangelism.

The evangelical view finds its roots in Scripture. The Bible is the record of God's redemptive acts in history, from Abraham to Christ and onward. It pictures God as the first and greatest of all evangelists, supremely interested in the redemption of His people and the establishment of His kingdom. It presents the Great Commission as the marching orders of Christ to His church.

Scriptures also portray all mankind as sinful, estranged from God, and in need of a Redeemer. All persons, therefore, need to be reconciled to God, to be "born again," and "be converted." Christ is presented as the one and only Saviour, who died for our sins and rose again to impart new life. Therefore, His name should be proclaimed among all nations. The salvation He offers is primarily deliverance from the guilt and bondage of sin.

In addition, the Gospels reveal that Christ was also concerned about the physical welfare of all persons. He healed the sick, fed the hungry, and ministered to the poor and despised. Likewise, missionaries have sought to provide education, medicine, shelter, and food through their schools, hospitals, orphanages, and relief work.

Those who follow the traditional view of mission see God as preparing people for the reception of the Gospel through a combination of the work of the Holy Spirit and environmental factors. They contend that we must look for such new historical opportunities where the Gospel finds receptive populations. We must recruit missionaries from east and west to secure a maximum number of disciples. We must concentrate on responsive areas. This incentive is the decisive motive for missionary recruitment in evangelical mission societies.

The traditional view is still accepted by the so-called faith missions, by mission boards of conservative churches, and by evangelical segments of mainline denominations.

The Ecumenical View
The second view of mission is called the ecumenical view, because it is primarily promoted by the World Council of

Churches, a worldwide Christian organization. This view does not find its motivation in Scriptures, but takes its cue from current history. It sees God at work in the sociopolitical revolution of the day, in the drive for justice, equality, freedom, and opportunity. The purpose of God's mission is to establish peace or the kingdom of God, which is interpreted as liberation from racial discrimination, unjust economic structures, and social and political oppression. It seeks to promote proper industrial relations and national development.

The following statement by a former mission board secretary is typical of the ecumenical view of mission:

> The arena of missionary activity will be the public sector. To liberate men from hunger, war, fear and human degradation; to confront political and social power groups that take advantage of the weak; and to cooperate with government in the private sector in serving mankind will be more and more the order of missionary priorities. (Tracey K. Jones, Jr., "A Look to the Future," *World Outlook*, April 1969, p. 34)

Those who hold this view are not satisfied with the humanitarian services of the church—running schools, hospitals, and orphanages, etc. They are more concerned about reordering the patterns of society and changing oppressive governments. They are more interested in liberating people from unjust structures that dehumanize them, that is, prevent them from enjoying their full human rights.

This modern view of mission contends that, in working toward the goal of liberation, God uses men and women both inside and outside the churches, people of faith and unfaith. He uses a Mao Tse-tung just as effectively as an E. Stanley Jones. The church is not God's principal instrument of redemption and ministry in the world. His primary relationship is to the world itself. The church's role in mission is to point to God at work in world history, to discover what He is doing, and then get involved in the action.

During the 1970s there were many ecumenical church leaders who hailed the Communist experiment in China as a great demonstration of liberation. They pointed out that there were no beggars, no prostitutes, and no flies in China. The people were delivered from outside dehumanizing forces. They had a new national self-esteem, a strong commitment to their cause, and faith in their future. In all this Mao Tse-tung was hailed as the "savior." What Christian missions had failed to bring about in China in 150 years, atheistic Communism had accomplished in just two or three decades.

The chief advocates of the ecumenical view of mission in the last twenty years or so have been the leaders of the World Council of Churches and, through their influence, staff members of the mainline denominational mission boards. At the fourth assembly of the WCC in Uppsala, Sweden, in 1968, a new theology of mission emerged. The council reversed the traditional order of God-church-world, to God-world-church. That is, instead of God working through His church in order to minister to the world, God carries on His work of liberation in the world, and the church is invited to be a partner in this activity along with other secular agents. The world sets the agenda, not the church. The focus of the council shifted from proclamation of the Gospel to attention to social, economic, and political issues. "Mission" was defined as "aid for development," with "humanization" as its goal. The council issued a call for mission societies to place the struggle for justice and development in the center of their activity.

The Commission on World Mission and Evangelism (the mission department of the WCC) carried this new theology of mission to further extremes at its meeting in Bangkok, Thailand, in 1973. Using the theme *Salvation Today*, the conference defined salvation in four dimensions:

1) Salvation works in the struggle for economic justice against the exploitation of people by people; 2) salvation works in the struggle for human dignity against political oppression of human beings by their fellow men; 3) salvation works in the solidarity against the alienation of person from person; 4) salvation works in the struggle of hope against despair in personal life.

The gathering went on to state that "salvation is the peace of people in Vietnam, independence in Angola, justice and reconciliation in Northern. Ireland, and release from the captivity of power in the North Atlantic community, or personal conversion in the release of a submerged society into hope, or of new lifestyles amidst corporate self-interest and lovelessness."

In other words, salvation means different things to different people in varying situations. It is not spiritual in nature, but social and political.

Contrasting the Two Views of Mission

We can readily see from all this that the modern view of mission constitutes a radical departure from the traditional view. We note the contrast in several different areas.

● The *traditional view* finds its roots in the *Scriptures,* in Christ's Great Commission to His church. It begins with God's redemptive acts in history (salvation history), from the call of Abraham to the coming of Christ. The *ecumenical view* finds its roots in the current world situation, and begins with God's liberating activity (world history) in the socio-political revolution of the day.

● In the *traditional view,* the emphasis is on *evangelism,* preaching the Gospel and establishing the church as the body of Christ. In the *ecumenical view* the emphasis is on involvement in the social and political issues that face us around the world.

● In the *traditional view,* the aim is *Christianization*—to produce a new people in Christ Jesus—Christlikeness. The mission is God-centered; Christ sets the agenda. In the *ecumenical view,* the aim is *humanization,* to enable people to enjoy their full humanity. The mission is man-centered; the world sets the agenda.

● The *traditional view* has a high view of the *spiritual nature of the church.* The church is God's instrument for redemption and service in the world. God is working through the church to reach the world. The *ecumenical view* has a *low view of the church.* It conceives the church as a purely sociological organization. The church is not closer to God than the world is. The only difference between the church and the rest of the world is that, because of her knowledge of the saving goal of history, the church now marches on ahead of the rest of humanity, as the vanguard in the movement toward the goal.

• The *traditional view* places the primary emphasis on the *vertical relationship* between persons and God. It contends that people must first be reconciled to God before they can be reconciled to one another. The emphasis is on conversion, calling people from unfaith to faith. The *ecumenical view* places the primary emphasis on the *horizontal relationship* between persons. It aims at producing radical changes in the structures of society. The goal is utopia, a perfect society in which there is no need for salvation. The emphasis is on dialogue with people of other religions and ideologies, so that there may be mutual understanding and cooperation.

Correcting the Two Views

Both the traditional and the ecumenical view of mission have strong and weak points. Each stands as a corrective and complement to the other.

The traditional view. Without a doubt the strength of the traditional view is that it understands the essence of mission as revealed in the Word of God. It clearly accepts the biblical statements about the sinfulness of humanity and God's eternal plan of salvation in Jesus Christ. People need to be born again, to be converted, to be reconciled to God. The danger, however, is for the traditional view to become too rigid in its theological position. It looks upon the world as getting worse and worse, headed for eventual destruction. World history has no positive meaning. Furthermore, Christ's return is imminent, so it is too late to change society. The objective of mission is to rescue as many people as possible from the present evil world and lead them into the safety of the ark, the church.

The tendency of such theological rigidity is for its advocates to overlook the great social problems here and now and take refuge in the hope of God's kingdom being established at some future date. They forget that the judgment of God is based not only on our response to the person of

Christ, but also on our response to the needs of people all around us (Matt. 25:31-46). Salvation is understood purely in the individual, vertical dimension, in personal relationship with God. It is not recognized that conversion has serious horizontal implications in transforming a person's relationship to others and in changing social structure. Evangelicals are correct in insisting that you cannot have a new society without new people, but they are naive in thinking that because individuals are born again, society will automatically change. Societal evil is far too subtle and entrenched for such a simple solution. Social reformation will take place only when there is a conscientious effort by God's redeemed people to change evil structures and stamp out injustice.

There is increasing evidence, however, that in recent years evangelicals have opened themselves up to the socio-ethical movement that permeates the whole of Christianity today. They have rediscovered the biblical passages that demand a concern about injustice and oppression and issue a call for sensitivity to human needs. The message of the prophets and the ministry of our Lord are prime examples of the biblical position. Evangelicals have also rediscovered their heritage and noted that the best traditions of evangelical piety have always combined revivalism and social reform. Noteworthy achievements of the past include the social changes resulting from the Wesleyan Revival in England in the eighteenth century, and the successful battle against slavery and the founding of the Red Cross in the nineteenth century. More recently, special statements issued by evangelical leaders meeting at Wheaton, Lausanne, and Chicago have clearly declared the urgent need for Christians to be involved in the social issues of the day. New organizations such as Evangelicals for Social Action, Bread for the World, Moral Majority, and the National Federation for Decency are all expressions of evangelical Christians coming together in a movement of faith and political conscience. Holding firmly to the priority of proclamation, these pronouncements and organizations call upon evangelical Christians to commit themselves to work "openly and firmly for racial equality, human freedom, and all forms of social justice throughout the world" (Wheaton Declaration).

The ecumenical view. The strength of the ecumenical view of mission lies in its genuine concern for the welfare of people and the betterment of society. This is highly commendable. The weakness of the position is that it is not the Scriptures, but history that reveals its standards for missionary activity. For the ecumenicals, the Bible and the teachings of Christ do not determine the direction of mission; the Scriptures are called upon only to support their preconceived view of mission. They contend that it is not what God has said and done in the Bible that sets the agenda; it is what God is supposedly doing in the world today that gives us our clue for action.

It is a serious mistake, however, to claim that all that is happening on the world scene today is the will or activity of God. It is naive to suggest that all revolutionary movements are signs of divine renewal. No doubt God is involved in some of the action, but we forget that the devil is also hard at work. Divine and demonic forces are locked in serious conflict around the world. Furthermore, even though in some cases the cause being promoted may be just, the methods employed to achieve the goal certainly cannot be condoned. God, who is Lord of history and is working through history, is also the Judge of history.

The preoccupation with social change in the ecumenical view leaves little or no room for evangelism. Concern for the spiritual needs of people and reaching the unevangelized areas of the world is for the most part lacking. "Presence" takes the place of proclamation. Christians should just be among people and quietly live out the Christian life in their midst, but they should not verbally witness for Christ or preach the Gospel. "Dialogue" takes the place of conversion. Christians should sit down with followers of other religions and ideologies and share back and forth about their beliefs. The aim of such dialogue is to help Christians and non-Christians understand each other more clearly and to become better friends, but not to change people's views and convert them to the Christian faith.

There is, of course, truth in both presence and dialogue, but when they are made substitutes for proclamation and conversion, then they become enemies of the truth. Presence is certainly necessary to proclamation. We must go to people, be among them, and identify ourselves with them in order to effectively witness to them. But there comes a time when we must speak the name and confront people with the claims of Christ. Dialogue is certainly a valuable aid to evangelism. It enables us to understand the beliefs of other people and be sympathetic with their position. Also, it makes our witness more genuine, for we have no right to expect other people to listen to us if we are not willing to listen to them. But dialogue should not dwindle down to mere conversation. It should clearly present the uniqueness of the Christian revelation with the hope of leading people to faith in Jesus Christ as Lord and Saviour.

The new emphasis on "humanization" (making people fully human) also poses some problems. It fails to realize that the most dehumanizing force in the world is one's sin. Sin robs people of their peace of mind, their moral standards of decency, and their own self-esteem. It causes people to be out of sorts with others and with themselves. Sin destroys all meaning and joy in living. It can turn persons into beasts. On the other hand, the greatest humanizing force in the world is the transforming power of the Lord Jesus Christ. When people are born of the Spirit, they become new persons in Christ. They not only partake of the divine nature, but they also become more fully human. They rise to their full human potential through the indwelling presence of the Holy Spirit. They become more and more like Christ, who, though He was completely divine, was also the most human person who ever lived.

Those who hold to the ecumenical view of mission need to return to the Bible and cease from turning half-truths into whole truths and from making substitutes for scriptural directives. They should recapture a genuine concern for evangelism and the spiritual needs of people.

FIVE

THE THEOLOGY OF LIBERATION

The theological basis for the current ecumenical view of mission is found in what is called liberation theology. Many books and articles have been written on the subject, and much heated debate has taken place. In some sections of the world, particularly Latin America, serious divisions have taken place within both the Protestant and the Roman Catholic churches over the question of liberation theology. Some claim it is God's truth for the present day; others state emphatically that it is the work of the devil. Most of the leaders of the World Council of Churches and staff members of the mainline mission boards have been greatly influenced by its concepts. To many evangelicals the very mention of liberation theology is like waving a red flag in front of a bull.

Because of the widespread impact of liberation theology today, it behooves us to take a good look at its main ideas. We need to view it with a critical yet sympathetic mind, to understand what are its values and its dangers. It is all too easy to dismiss liberation theology as pure heresy and fail to see that it might be saying something important that we need to consider seriously.

We note at the outset that liberation theology is a very complex system of thought. Most books written by its advocates are highly sophisticated and difficult for the ordinary lay person without a theological background to understand. We shall seek to make the discussion simple, using as little technical language as possible. Furthermore, it must be pointed out that there is no one universal version, but many varieties of liberation theology. There are, for example, continental versions. There are Latin American, Asian, and African expressions of liberation theology. There is also black theology, as developed in Africa and in North America. Then there is native American theology and feminist theology here in the United States. In addition, there are individual versions of liberation theology held by different persons living in the same country. Some advocates are politically moderate; others are radical and even Marxist in their views. So it is not proper to indiscriminately lump together all of the expressions of liberation theology into one neat packet. However, all these versions share certain common concerns and emphases, which makes our task somewhat simpler. To these common concepts, especially as defined in the Latin American context, we now turn our attention.

Liberation theology had its origin and is most articulate in Latin America. Ruben Alves (Brazilian Presbyterian) and Richard Shaull (American Presbyterian) were among the first ecumenical Protestant theologians to give enthusiastic support to its ideas. More recently Emilio Castro (Uruguayan Methodist) and Jose Miguez Bonino (Argentinian Methodist) have been the key Protestant spokesmen. Among the chief Roman Catholic exponents of the theology of liberation are Hugo Assman (Brazilian), Juan Luis Segundo (Uruguayan), and Gustavo Gutierrez (Peruvian). The latter's book, *A Theology of Liberation* (1973), is considered the classic text on the subject.

The Main Concepts of Liberation Theology

Emphasis on situation. Liberation theology originated in response to the severe social problems found throughout Latin America—hunger, poverty, lack of education, disease, and political injustice. People suffer and die daily because of the miserable conditions in which they live. Malnutrition and sickness claim hundreds of thousands of children. Adults live in a pit of ignorance, vice, corruption, and exploitation. The sad part is that though the church has been a major force on the continent for over 450 years, it has done very little to solve these problems. In fact, it has often taken the side of the rich and elite against the poor and oppressed. It has helped to maintain the status quo. Instead of permeating and transforming society, the church has become like a fortress or an ark, unrelated to the world and its needs. Theologians have had an ivory-tower mentality, engaging themselves in mere mental exercises and doctrinal disputes.

Reacting negatively to all this, some people in the church have developed a new theology that they believe offers clear and forceful solutions to the suffering prevalent in Latin American society. Instead of going back to the Word of God and finding biblical principles to apply to the conditions, they have looked at the problems and formulated a theology to fit the situation. This constitutes a whole new approach to theology. Instead of proceeding from Bible to situation, it goes from situation to Bible. Thus, the liberationists have a tendency to read into the Bible certain interpretations by which they justify their actions.

Emphasis on "praxis." A favorite word in liberation theology is *praxis,* the Greek word for "practice." Liberation theology is interested in doing, not thinking; in applied truth, not abstract theory. It is concerned with results. "What's the use," it asks, "of sitting around studying the truth and formulating correct doctrinal statements if it doesn't change conditions in society?" Liberation theology claims to be practical; it is to produce results and change society. Thought and action, liberationists insist, are inseparable. Thinking should lead to doing. In fact, one cannot really know the truth until he puts it into practice. Truth is not pure thought, but thought in action. The emphasis is on *doing* theology, not *studying* theology. Advocates of liberation theology say that if your theology is not getting the job done, then change your theology.

Emphasis on this world. Liberationists are concerned about this world as contrasted to the afterworld. They concentrate on the present, not the future. They say that the church's preoccupation with the world to come is a cop-out, an attempt to escape responsibility for the problems of our day. They deny the claim that the wrongs of this world will be righted only in the next world. Liberationists join with

Karl Marx in saying that "religion is the opiate of the people." It forces people to meekly accept their deplorable conditions in this world and hope for "pie in the sky." It keeps people from revolting against the status quo, when rightfully they should revolt.

Liberation theology is thus a theology of hope for the world. Its goal is to produce a utopia here and now, where there will be complete racial and sexual equality, harmonious industrial and national relationships, and justice and opportunity for all.

Emphasis on liberation. When asked what is the central theme of the Christian faith, liberationists answer emphatically with one word—*liberation!* The concept of justice plays an important part in their thinking. They are greatly concerned about oppression and poverty and believe that this is also God's greatest concern. God, they claim, can be known only in the struggle for justice. In their view of the Bible, God breaks into human history to liberate the oppressed. The great example always cited is the Exodus story, in which the people of Israel were delivered from Egyptian slavery. The oppressed people of the world are identified with the Israelites in their deliverance. "The liberation of Israel was a political action," say the liberationists.

What is wrong with oppression? It is a denial of liberty. And what is the proof that liberty has been denied? The fact that humanity suffers from inequality. Liberation theologians point to the enormous distance between rich and poor in Latin America and the inequality between the affluent and the undeveloped nations. All this inequality is not an inevitable fact of nature, nor is it the will of God. The poor were *made* poor by the social system, particularly capitalism as expressed in the multinational corporations.

What then is salvation? According to liberation theology, salvation is liberation from injustice and exploitation, from everything that prevents us from being "truly human." Although liberationists acknowledge personal sin, they ascribe its existence to oppressive social and political structures; these alone produce and perpetuate it. Guilt is primarily social. Consequently, no deliverance from individual sin is possible except through the overthrow of the unjust structures that are the root cause.

Conversion, according to liberationists, is the act of committing oneself to the struggle for justice and to the liberation of the poor and oppressed. If a rich man is to be helpful in this process, he must become poor and identify himself with the oppressed, becoming one of them.

View of the church. Liberationists have a very low view of the church. In fact, they are more concerned about the world than the church. In their opinion, the church is not the community of those who have been reconciled to God through faith in Jesus Christ. It is rather all those who are willing to participate in the struggle for liberation. It is the duty of the church to develop among the poor, oppressed masses an awareness of their plight and the realization that their status can be changed. The church needs to keep reinterpreting the Bible in the light of the continual changes in our society. Only by doing this can it have an effective ministry to people.

Liberation theologians look upon Christ primarily as a political Messiah, a liberator of politically and economically oppressed people. Thus, the liberationists' view of Christ is more like what the Jews expected Him to be, rather than what He claimed for Himself.

Influence of Marxism. In the liberation movement there has been a general acceptance of Marxist concepts, especially as a method of analyzing and solving the social problems of the day. Liberationists believe that Karl Marx understood more about the dynamics of history than theologians and that his analysis of the class struggle is essentially correct. Gutierrez, the chief Roman Catholic exponent, claims that Marxism is science and Christianity is faith.

However, we cannot charge liberationists with adopting Marxism uncritically. After all, Communists are atheists, while Christians believe in God. Liberation theologians have done some evaluating and sifting of the issues. They reject the wholesale embracing of Marxism as contrary to the Christian faith. They maintain that they accept Marxism merely as a scientific analysis of the way that economics and politics operate in society.

Latin American liberationists are committed to restructuring society along the lines of socialism. They feel that capitalism is largely responsible for the mess we are in, and socialism is the best way out. Many engage in violent revolutionary action to achieve the goal. They justify their use of force by arguing that violence is initiated by those who oppress, exploit, and fail to recognize others as persons, not by those who are oppressed, exploited, and unrecognized.

Positive Values of Liberation Theology

We see from this discussion that liberation theology does have some positive values. We need to keep an open mind to these values but at the same time be on the lookout for the dangers.

Evangelicals have no quarrel with the goal of human liberation. On the contrary, with our biblical doctrine of human dignity, everything that dehumanizes should arouse our indignant opposition, and everything that humanizes, our enthusiastic support. The situation in Latin America and other countries is indeed desperate and is a challenge for the church to become involved in meeting the needs of the common masses.

We welcome the insistence on *praxis* (practice), an active Christian involvement on behalf of the poor and oppressed. For as James put it, "Faith without works is dead" (James 2:20, NKJV), and Paul wrote that faith works through love (Gal. 5:6). John in his epistle admonishes us to love not in word, but in deed and in truth (1 John 3:18). Faith is not just a head trip, merely believing certain things. Faith must be expressed in action. Doctrine must end in doing.

Liberation theology challenges us to maintain a more holistic view of people. Though liberationists are prone to neglect people's spiritual needs because of their emphasis on physical and social needs, they are reminding us that the human person is a unit—soul, mind, and body—and that we should not separate "spiritual" from "physical" but should minister to the total needs of individuals. Liberation theologians have been able to add an important dimension to the interpretation of scriptural concepts, including peace, justice, righteousness, kingdom, and poverty.

Liberation theology has reminded us that sin is not only

personal but also societal. There are individual sins and corporate sin. The latter resides in the unjust structures of society that make it difficult for individuals to be the persons they ought to be. Liberationists insist that discipleship is not only personal and private, but social and public as well. To seek to "save" individuals without transforming society is like putting a Band-Aid on an abscess without lancing the sore. We should all participate responsibly in the political process to fight injustice and oppression. To all of this we say a hearty "Amen!"

Negative Aspects of Liberation Theology

In reacting against a very narrow conservative type of Christian theology, liberation theology has overreacted and gone to extremes in the opposite direction.

The first fallacy of liberation theology is its *overemphasis on liberation.* Liberty is not the central theme of the Christian faith. Consider, for example, the story of the Exodus, which is a favorite passage of liberationists. Note what the Lord commanded Moses to say to Pharaoh: "Let My people go that they might serve Me" (Ex. 8:1, NKJV). The object of liberty was freedom to serve and glorify God. The people of Israel were shifted from servitude to Pharaoh to servitude to God. Instead of leaving them to their own devices, God gave them the moral law, details of worship, and even government.

We are disturbed with the liberationists' *view of salvation and conversion.* In the Bible salvation is clearly portrayed as reconciliation with God, deliverance from the guilt and power of sin. Conversion is a turning around, away from one's self to God. Liberation theology defines salvation in collective terms (liberation of society) to the virtual exclusion of individual redemption. It equates salvation with liberation from economic and political oppression. Conversion is not a turning to God but a turning to our fellow human beings. The essential requirement is no longer faith in Jesus Christ but simply active participation in human liberation. Thus, even an atheistic ideology such as Marxism, which claims to produce economic and political liberation, can be viewed as a contribution to the "redemption of society." This undercuts the uniqueness of Christ and the necessity of a personal experience with Christ. In so doing, it removes the motive for evangelism.

We evangelicals cannot be satisfied with the liberationists' *understanding of the person and ministry of Jesus Christ.* They view Christ as a political Messiah rather than a spiritual Saviour. They portray the Master as a political revolutionary who condones the use of violence to overthrow injustice. Some liberation theologians redefine Christian "love" to mean participation in the class struggle on behalf of the oppressed peoples. Others turn the crucifixion of Jesus Christ into a political event rather than a sacrifice to redeem humanity from sin. All this constitutes a serious perversion of the Christian faith.

Liberation theology has *a very shallow view of the tragedy of sin.* It overemphasizes the societal aspect of sin and sees sin as residing primarily in evil social and political structures. The doctrine of original sin plays no part in the thinking of liberationists. They seem to forget the innate selfishness and rebellion of human nature. They give the impression that if you straighten out the crooked structures of society, everything will be all right. In fact, some extreme advocates of liberation theology seem to imply that once this utopia on earth has been established, there will be no need for individual salvation. But history shows that often when an oppressive regime is overthrown, another equally oppressive regime takes its place. It's like taking out one bunch of sinners and putting another in its place. The boot is still there, holding people down, but the foot is different, perhaps a different color. The Bible teaches clearly that sin is both in the individual and in society. It is entrenched in the human heart, and nothing but radical surgery by the grace of God can bring the remedy.

There is in liberation theology a strong *tendency to ignore or marginalize the church.* The distinction between the church and the world, between faith and unfaith, is blurred. The church is not so much the fellowship of the redeemed as it is the base for liberation activity. True, the church has its frailties and is at times irrelevant, but we are not willing to give up the church. It is not dispensable; it is vital, essential.

The Bible pictures the church as the body of Christ, His point of contact with the world, His instrument for redemption and service in the world. It also portrays the church as the bride of Christ, called to be holy and to enter into a love relationship with her Lord. The reason for the impotence found in many segments of the church today is that it has allowed itself to become too much like the world. The church must certainly be *in* the world, but never *of* the world. Instead of neglecting the church or writing it off as a thing of the past, we should pray and work for the renewal of the church. Jesus said that He Himself would build the church, and the gates of hell would not prevail against it.

Finally, we evangelicals are deeply disturbed by *the influence of Marxist philosophy* on the theology of liberationists. This has produced serious results: the preoccupation with sociopolitical issues to the neglect of evangelism, a dependence on the social sciences rather than on the Word of God, a purely materialistic view of life, and a tendency toward humanism and secularism. (*Humanism* is the dependence on human efforts and wisdom to the exclusion of God; *secularism* is the attitude that religion and faith should not enter into public life.) This leads to a faulty view of the kingdom.

In the Bible the central meaning of the kingdom of God is the reign of God, which will result in a society of fellowship and justice among all people. But the liberationists perceive the kingdom in terms of a utopian society of fellowship, love, and justice without considering its cause—the reign of God. So in essence the kingdom of God becomes the kingdom of man, built by human efforts. God is not necessary. Here is where the camel of atheism pokes its nose into the tent of Christendom. Little or nothing is said about the kingdom to come. The Scriptures clearly teach that the kingdom is brought about by God Himself and is both present and future. In the present the reign of God is limited (to persons and areas where it is acknowledged), and we are called to be active partners with God in its establishment. The universal and complete kingdom of God will be established at the future return of Christ in power and glory.

We must also challenge the liberationists' *willingness to*

use violence to achieve their ends. Is violence and revolution the only way out? Is this the Christian answer? Do two wrongs make a right? Does the violence of the oppressor justify the violence of the oppressed? Violence usually leads to more violence and often to the breakdown of law and order.

So it can be seen that the greatest danger of liberation theology is that it results in a new kind of works righteousness. *Praxis,* or doing, is set against faith. It doesn't matter so much what you believe, just so you act right (by participating in the struggle for liberation and justice). The kingdom is brought in by human effort and wisdom. God may be a help, but He is not essential. This does away with the basic doctrine of justification by faith as taught in the Word of God. Liberationists say we are to seek justice in society without justification in the individual. And this strikes at the very heart of the Christian faith.

Concluding Remarks

There are four types of revolution. *Violent revolution* merely reverses the order or role of the oppressor and the oppressed. Those oppressed become the oppressors. *Pseudorevolution* deals only with fringe matters, not basic problems. *Nonviolent revolution,* like the ones led by Mahatma Gandhi and Martin Luther King, is another. Usually the leaders are killed, but it has a greater impact on society. Finally there is the *new order in Christ,* which results in not just major repairs on a dying social order but evangelistic Christian reformation. The best example of this is the Wesleyan movement that saved England from a bloody revolution. Revolution must be remedial, for the good of all.

Revolution means sudden, radical change. In this sense, the Christian faith and the grace of God are revolutionary, for they produce a drastic change in the inner life. New persons are needed to produce a new world. Biblical concepts thus save us from cheap ideas of revolution. The trouble with liberation theology is that it is not radical enough; it doesn't go to the root cause of the matter.

Jesus was a revolutionary in conflict with the existing social order, but He was not a political revolutionary. He rejected the popular concept of the Messiah. He was not a political adventurer. He accepted the state and opposed revolt. He was a suffering servant. Jesus, however, was a religious revolutionary, changing concepts of religion and transforming lives. Even today He cleanses cultures from that which is contrary to God's will and nature.

The pseudo-revolutionary falls prey to power, prestige, and self-centeredness. Jesus, however, was a genuine revolutionary, refusing to be molded by the environment.

How can the church best help revolution? By providing regenerated leaders with the moral fiber to give the revolution permanency and help keep it from corruption by speaking to the moral implications of social issues with a prophetic voice.

SIX EVANGELISM AND SOCIAL ACTION

I remember when I was in college listening to Dr. H.C. Morrison tell about calling on the devil one day. (He didn't explain why he visited the devil.) When he arrived, the devil said, "Here, have a seat." Dr. Morrison turned to see a large block of ice. When Dr. Morrison refused to sit on the ice seat, the devil then offered him a second seat, and Dr. Morrison turned to see a sizzling hot stove. In concluding the story, he told us, "I discovered those are the only two seats the devil has. He will either try to freeze you out or burn you up."

This is a crude but forceful illustration of the strong temptation prevalent among Christians to go to extremes. For a long time the church will neglect a certain facet of Christian doctrine, and then some people will come along and take that facet and make it the whole Gospel. Then there is a reaction to the extreme position, followed by another reaction to the reaction. And often it is an overreaction. To keep all aspects of the Christian message in proper balance, to preach a whole Gospel to the total person, is certainly a most difficult, yet essential, task of the church.

In recent years there has been an enormous amount of ferment and debate in Christian circles on the issue of evangelism and social action. Some contend that evangelism is the primary concern of the church and so either downgrade or completely neglect social action. Then some argue that social action is the chief task of the church and thus tend to

65

make it a substitute for evangelism. There has been a tragic dichotomy between evangelism and social concern. The former is interested in souls; the latter, in soap and soup.

What is the way out of this situation? Is it an either-or proposition? Do we have to make a choice between evangelism and social action, or can we unite the two in a holistic approach?

The Teaching of Scriptures

A careful study of the Gospels reveals that evangelism and social action are two facets of the Christian faith. They are like the two sides of a coin.

To begin with, look at the commandments of our Lord. Note first the Great Commission as recorded by all four Gospel writers. There can be no doubt that the Matthew, Mark, and Luke versions of the commission place the emphasis on evangelism. "Go therefore and make disciples of all nations, baptizing them . . . teaching them" (Matt. 28:19-20, KJV). "Go into all the world and preach the Gospel to the whole creation" (Mark 16:15). "Repentance and forgiveness of sins should be preached in His name to all nations. . . . You are witnesses of these things" (Luke 24:47-48). The combined emphasis seems clear. It is placed on preaching, witnessing, and making disciples.

We must not, however, overlook the commission as given in John's Gospel: "As the Father has sent Me, even so I send you" (John 20:21). Here Christ deliberately made His mission the model of ours. Our understanding of the church's mission must follow from our understanding of Christ's mission. Why and how did the Father send the Son?

Jesus made it very clear in His public ministry that He "came not to be served but to serve, and to give His life as a ransom for many" (Mark 10:45). On another occasion He said: "I am among you as one who serves" (Luke 22:27). The giving of His life as a ransoming sin offering was a sacrifice He alone could offer, but this was to be the climax of a life of service. We cannot go to the cross as Jesus did—for He alone is Saviour—but there is a sense in which we must take up our cross daily and follow Him. His cross was the propitiation for sin; our cross is the principle for service. So as Jesus gave

Himself in selfless service for others, so must we. His service took a variety of forms, according to the needs of people. He preached, proclaiming the good news of the kingdom of God. He taught, showing how to enter the kingdom and how it would spread. But He served in deed as well as in word. Studying His ministry, it is impossible to separate His works from His words. He healed the sick, washed dirty feet, fed the hungry, comforted the sad, and preached to the poor.

Now Christ, the sent one, turns around and sends us. Our mission, like His, is one of service. As Paul said, Christ emptied Himself of all His prerogatives and took upon Himself the form of a servant, and this same mind-set is to be in us (Phil. 2:5-8). We must be willing to renounce status and assume the role of a servant. Instead of reaching for the top, we are to take up the towel. All the symbols of the Christian faith—manger, basin, and cross—emphasize this truth. So with Christ as our model we should go forth to proclaim the Gospel and serve others. John Stott suggests that "it is in our servant role that we can find the right synthesis of evangelism and social action. For both should be for us, as they undoubtedly were for Christ, authentic expressions of the love that serves" (*Christian Mission in the Modern World*, InterVarsity Press, p. 24).

We must note another important aspect of Christ's mission that is essential for ours: in order to serve, He was sent *into the world*. In His priestly prayer He said clearly, "As Thou didst send Me into the world, so I have sent them into the world" (John 17:18); Jesus did not come as a fly-by-night angel or a foreign visitor. He took upon Himself our humanity and went through the whole gamut of human experiences. He identified with our poverty: He was born in a stable. He identified with our toil: He worked at a carpenter's bench. He identified with our basic human needs: He knew what it was to be hungry, thirsty, and tired. He identified with human culture and language: He was born a Jew and spoke Aramaic. He identified with our temptations: He was "in every respect . . . tempted as we are, yet without sin" (Heb. 4:15). He identified with our suffering: He was called "a man of sorrows and acquainted with grief" (Isa. 53:3). He even tasted our death: He died on the cross.

And now Christ sends us into the world to identify with the culture, language, pains, aspirations, sorrows, and needs of a particular people. We are to be vulnerable as He was. The principle of incarnation (the Word becoming flesh) must be a model for our service, as much as the principle of the crucifixion (the giving of one's self). This means we cannot fulfill our mission with just a handout; we must actually give our hands. We cannot be satisfied with a hit-and-run type of evangelism; we must stay long enough to involve ourselves deeply in the lives of the people, in their problems and needs. We cannot yell at people from a distance; we must get close enough to listen, see their tears, and feel their heartbeats.

It is clear that the Great Commission gives place for both evangelism and social action. The first three Gospels emphasize the importance of preaching and making disciples, while the fourth Gospel implies, in modeling the church's mission on Christ's, that we are sent into the world to serve. This humble service will include both words and works, a concern for both physical and spiritual needs. It is a concern for souls as well as soap and soup.

This truth becomes even more evident when we take a look at the Great Commandment Jesus gave to His disciples, the command to "love your neighbor as yourself" (Mark 12:31). Our tendency is to give all our attention to the Great Commission and to overlook the Great Commandment. We act as if the commission to disciple all nations were the only instruction Jesus left us. In reality we must observe *all* that Jesus taught, and not just a part.

Like the Great Commission, so also the Great Commandment implies the need for both evangelism and social action. If we truly love people as Christ loved them, then we will seek to minister to their total needs. We shall, without doubt, share with them the good news that God loves them and Christ died for them. How can we possibly claim to love our neighbors if we know the Gospel and keep it from them? Witnessing thus becomes an integral part of the Christian life. It is equally true that if we genuinely love our neighbors, we will not stop with evangelism. To use the words of John Stott, "Our neighbour is neither a bodyless soul that we should love only his soul, nor a soulless body that we should care for its welfare alone, nor even a body-soul isolated from society. God created man, who is my neighbour, a body-soul-in-community" (*Christian Mission in the Modern World*, pp. 29–30). Therefore, if we love our neighbor as God made him, we must inevitably be concerned for his total welfare, the good of his soul, his body, and his community.

Jesus dramatically taught us that concern for both spiritual and physical welfare is essential to Christian life and mission. This is clearly seen in Luke's Gospel, chapter 10, where we find, back-to-back, two important records. The first is the dialogue between Christ and a certain lawyer (vv. 25-37). The latter asked Jesus, "What shall I do to inherit eternal life?" Jesus affirmed that the answer lay in the commands, "Love the Lord your God with all your heart, and with all your soul, and with all your strength, and with all your mind; and your neighbor as yourself." Then when the lawyer asked, "Who is my neighbor?" Jesus told the beautiful story of the Good Samaritan. A man was beaten up and left half dead on the roadside. Two men came along, a priest and a Levite— both religious men. But they passed by, without even lifting a little finger to help the poor man in the ditch. They were in too much of a rush to make it to the temple in Jerusalem for the evening service. Then along came a Samaritan, a person of a different social grouping, and in compassion he stopped to minister to the destitute traveler. What Jesus was saying in all this was that worship without service is a farce. Our faith must be expressed in deeds.

Immediately after the parable, Luke records a dialogue between Jesus and Martha of Bethany (vv. 38-42). Jesus was visiting the home of Mary and Martha, two sisters. Mary sat at the Master's feet and listened to His teaching. "But Martha was distracted with much serving." She was an activist, running back and forth between the kitchen and the parlor. Then Jesus gently rebuked her, saying, "Martha, you are anxious and troubled about many things; one thing is need-ful. Mary has chosen the good portion." In essence He was saying that service without worship is equally a farce.

The combined force of these two dialogues is that both worship and service are essential; concern for both spiritual and physical matters is necessary. In like manner, evangelism and social action are both essential ingredients of the Christian mission. We must be concerned for the total welfare of humankind. We must minister to the total needs of all persons.

I had a conversation with Bishop Lesslie Newbigin in Madras, South India, several years ago, and the bishop gave a forceful illustration of this point. He said: "The Gospel is like a pair of scissors. You cannot cut anything with just one blade; you must have two. Furthermore, if the rivet gets loose and the two blades pull apart, again you do not have a cutting edge. The two blades must be close together to be effective. In the same way," explained the bishop, "the Gospel has two components—evangelism and social action. You cannot have a cutting edge in society without the two. Furthermore, they must be kept in close relationship, or again, you will not make an impact on society."

Then Bishop Newbigin went on to give a second illustration. He said, "The Gospel may also be compared to a seesaw. There are two principles involved in a seesaw. The first is that it must be on center, otherwise it will tip to one side. Second, it must have proper balance. If a person weighing 250 pounds sits on one side, and a person weighing just 75 pounds sits on the other, again the seesaw will go down on one side. In the same way, the two sides of the Gospel seesaw—evangelism and social action—must be on center, and that center is Christ. If evangelism is not centered on Him, then it can degenerate to a mad scramble for numbers or a selfish scheme for making money. If social action is not centered on Christ, then it can become a paternalistic handout or even a scheme for violence. Furthermore, there must be a proper balance between evangelism and social action, otherwise the one will tend to exclude or become a substitute for the other."

The bishop's sound advice forces us to raise an important question: what is the relationship between evangelism and social action within our total Christian responsibility? If we concede that we have no right either to concentrate on evangelism to the exclusion of social action or to make social action a substitute for evangelism, we still need to define the relation between the two.

Relation Between Evangelism and Social Action

To put it briefly, evangelism and social action are equally important but genuinely distinct aspects of the total mission of the church, yet inseparably interrelated.

Evangelism and social action are distinct from each other. Evangelism is not social action and social action is not evangelism. Evangelism is announcing the good news of Jesus Christ. It proclaims justification by faith, the forgiveness of sins, the gift of the Holy Spirit, a personal relationship with Jesus Christ. All who have not been reborn in Jesus Christ, whether they are in or outside the church, need to be evangelized. Only persons can respond to this good news. It is confusing the issue to talk about evangelizing political or economic structures. Multinational corporations or social institutions cannot repent, enter into a personal relationship with Jesus Christ, or join the church. Of course these systems need to be changed, but passing a good law or transforming an unjust society is not the same thing as leading an individual into a personal relationship with the Saviour.

In like manner, social action is not evangelism. Social action is the attempt to meet physical human needs and reform society. It has to do with feeding the hungry, healing the sick, teaching illiterates, and so on. It is concerned with such issues as poverty, injustice, oppression, and war. Social action seeks to reform inhuman political, social, and economic structures. We confuse the issue when we claim to have evangelized people because we have alleviated their hunger or restored to them their basic human rights.

Evangelism is preaching the Gospel; social action is serving and reforming society. They are distinct and independent of each other. Each stands on its own feet. Neither is a means to the other or even a manifestation of the other. For each is an end in itself, an expression of unfeigned love.

However, we must be quick to add that evangelism and social action are closely interrelated and cannot be separated. As Martin Luther King showed us, they are partners in the wider mission of the church. As such, they belong to each other and support one another. Both are responses to human need. It is the nature of the need that determines the response. If we see spiritual need (sin, guilt, lostness), then evangelism springs into action and we share the good news of the Gospel (forgiveness, peace, reconciliation). If we see disease or ignorance or bad housing, then social activism springs into action, and we seek the medical, educational, or economic resources to meet those needs. To see need and to possess the remedy compels the Christian to act in love. Whether the action will be evangelistic, social, or political depends on the nature of the need.

Jesus is our model in this regard. To the sinner, He offered forgiveness. To the despised, He offered hope. To the fearful, He offered peace. To the hungry, He offered bread; to the sick, wholeness. Jesus challenged the status quo whenever it was wrong. He challenged the legalism of the Pharisees with His call to pure motives and inner purity. He challenged the rulers' lust for power with His call to servant leadership. He upset the male population with His discourse on divorce. He summoned the political zealots to love their enemies. He broke social custom by treating women as equals. He challenged the economic establishment to forgive the debtor and minister to the poor.

And now a final question: granted that evangelism and social action are distinct and equally significant, does the one have priority over the other? We need to come at this question of priority from different angles. This is a complex problem and requires some explanation.

There is first the fact of *innate priority.* Eternal spiritual verities naturally take precedence over temporal physical welfare. Jesus plainly taught that it is better to lose the whole world than forfeit eternal life. Gaining eternal life and living in the presence of Jesus is more important than bread, housing, or justice. Then, there is the question of *logical priority.* If we want Christian social responsibility, we must have Christians; if we want a better society, we must have better people. So there is an inherent priority in evangelism.

But there is also a *temporal* or *situational priority.* Must we always proclaim the Gospel before we help hungry people? No biblical Christian would agree to that. When people are starving, they need food, not a sermon. When people are recovering from an earthquake or tornado, they need shelter and clothing. Furthermore, there are some countries, like Nepal, where the authorities have permitted Christian missionaries to come and establish hospitals and schools, but have forbidden them to evangelize the people. The missionaries didn't say, "Our first business is to preach the Gospel. If we can't do that, we are not coming in to heal and teach." Constrained by the love of Christ, they entered the country to minister to the needs of the people. So priority sometimes depends on the situation.

Then there is the question of *vocational priority*. If evangelism has a built-in priority because of its very nature, must all Christians, regardless of their profession, spend most of their time and energy in evangelism? No. Mark Hatfield is a United States Senator and rightfully spends most of his time in politics (though he seizes the opportunity to witness for Christ by word and deed whenever it arises). Billy Graham is an evangelist and rightfully spends most of his time in conducting evangelistic campaigns and preaching the Gospel (though he speaks out on social issues whenever necessary). Some people are especially called by God to serve Him by means of social action, like Mother Teresa of India. Others are called by God to serve Him in the evangelistic field, like astronaut James Irwin. Some people have special talents in the area of social activism and find fulfillment and joy in serving the public sector. Some are gifted in evangelism and serve most effectively by ministering to the spiritual needs of people. Some church members delight in working with the committee on social concerns; others prefer to serve on the committee for evangelism and missions. In either case, the evangelist should recognize the calling and gifts of the social activist and give that person full support, and vice versa. It is when the body of Christ recognizes the various functions of its members and works in perfect harmony that it is best able to fulfill its mission in the world and bring glory to God.

Perhaps one of the finest statements on the nature of evangelism and social action, and the relation between the two, is found in a document called the Lausanne Covenant. This is a doctrinal declaration that came out of the strategic International Congress on World Evangelization, held in Lausanne, Switzerland in July 1974 and sponsored by Dr. Billy Graham. The covenant expresses a consensus of the mind and mood of the 2,700 delegates who were present at the Congress, representing more than 150 nations.

The fourth paragraph of the Lausanne Covenant begins with a definition and goes on to describe the context of evangelism, namely what must precede and follow it.

To evangelize is to spread the good news that Jesus Christ died for our sins and was raised from the dead according to the Scriptures, and that as the reigning Lord he now offers the forgiveness of sins and the liberating gift of the Holy Spirit to all who repent and believe. Our Christian presence in the world is indispensable to evangelism, and so is that kind of dialogue whose purpose is to listen sensitively in order to understand. But evangelism itself is the proclamation of the historical, biblical Christ as Savior and Lord, with a view to persuading people to come to him personally and so be reconciled to God. In issuing the Gospel invitation we have no liberty to conceal the cost of discipleship. Jesus still calls all who would follow him to deny themselves, take up their cross, and identify themselves with his new community. The results of evangelism include obedience to Christ, incorporation into his church and responsible service in the world.

Paragraph 5 makes the following statement concerning Christian social responsibility:

We affirm that God is both the Creator and the Judge of all men. We therefore should share his concern for justice and reconciliation throughout human society and for the liberation of men from every kind of oppression. Because mankind is made in the image of God, every person, regardless of race, religion, color, culture, sex or age, has an intrinsic dignity because of which he should be respected and served, not exploited. Here too we express penitence both for our neglect and for having sometimes regarded evangelism and social concern as mutually exclusive. Although reconciliation with man is not reconciliation with God, nor is social action evangelism, nor is political liberation salvation, nevertheless we affirm that evangelism and socio-political involvement are both part of our Christian duty. For both are necessary expressions of our doctrines of God and man, our love for our neighbor and our obedience to Jesus Christ. The message of salvation implies also a message of judgment upon every form of alienation, oppression and discrimination, and we should not be afraid to denounce evil and injustice wherever they exist. When people receive Christ they are born again into his kingdom and must seek not only to exhibit but also to spread its righteousness in the midst of an unrighteous world. The salvation we claim should be transforming us in the totality of our personal and social responsibilities. Faith without works is dead.

In summary, we must reiterate that there is no contradiction between evangelism and social action. Both are essential components of the Christian mission. Each is distinct and stands on its own feet, but neither can exist apart from the other. Evangelism and social action are partners in the total mission of the church and should complement each other with their ministries. We must remember the good advice of Bishop Lesslie Newbigin: keep on center and maintain the balance!

PART THREE

REVOLUTIONARY TIMES—What Kind of World Do We Live In?

The world all around us has changed drastically in the last few decades. Christian missionaries today work in a far different environment than did their predecessors. We have witnessed the death of colonialism and the rise of nationalism; political independence coming to many nations, but loss of individual freedom in some; an alarming increase in world population; a mad race to the cities; revival of the non-Christian religions; and the widening gulf between rich nations and poor nations. All these changes have made a serious impact on the Christian mission. The church must learn to adjust its strategy to the new situation but still be faithful to its God-given mission.

SEVEN

OUR POLITICAL WORLD

During the 1930s a popular Broadway play, *Green Pastures,* portrayed heaven as imagined by a black preacher of the old days. One scene shows God, presiding at His desk, looking down at the earth, disturbed by what is taking place. He dispatches His chief secretary, the angel Gabriel, to find out what all the commotion is about. When Gabriel returns, the Lord asks him "What's going on down there?" Gabriel replies, "Lawd, everything that's a-nailed down is a-comin' loose!"

This is an accurate description of the times in which we live. Everything is a-comin' loose. To be a missionary in this, the last quarter of the twentieth century, is quite different from what it was in the beginning of the century. The missionary of today must be prepared for life in a revolutionary world. Sweeping changes are taking place in every area of human life: political, social, economic, and religious. Christians on the home front must have an awareness about the kind of world in which their ambassadors are serving. They should have both accurate knowledge and balanced understanding of the current affairs that greatly affect the life and ministry of the missionary.

Nature of the World Revolution
Basically, the world revolution is simply that of the common person, in the grip of two all-powerful ideas. Victor Hugo

said years ago, "All the armies in the world cannot withstand the power of an idea whose time has come." This implies that an idea can be rolling around in the minds of people for a long time before its supreme hour dawns, but when its time comes, not even an army can turn back its tide. Common people around the world are caught by the irresistible force of two great ideas whose time has come. The first idea is that everyone, everywhere, is entitled to the basic things of life. This means that billions of people in Asia, the Middle East, Africa, and South America who for many years have been saying in one way or another, "My disease, poverty, hunger, ignorance, nakedness, and hopelessness are the result of my fate. My misfortune is my *karma*, my *kismet*, God's will for me and my children," are not saying that any longer. Instead they are saying, "No, this is not God's will. It is my right to have food, clothing, education, health, a decent home, a higher standard of living. It belongs to me and my children, and I shall have it at all costs." Someone has called this the "revolution of rising expectations."

The second idea is that all persons, regardless of color, race, or nationality, are of equal worth and thus deserve an equal opportunity in life. No one is willing to be treated as a "second-rate citizen" anymore. No one is willing to receive lower wages than a coworker who works the same job for the same number of hours. This new sense of human dignity has given rise to the anti-caste movement in India, the civil rights movement in the United States, and the feminist movement around the world.

These two ideas have existed for a long time, but only in recent years have they reached the fullness of time. We can hear the "thunder of bare feet in the palace" across the world. Since the end of World War II, these two ideas have modified more thinking, reshaped more institutions, given birth to more new nations, changed more customs, and torn loose more things formerly nailed down than any other such movement in all of history.

What is the origin of this worldwide revolution? Some people in the United States seem to think it is Communism. They glibly say, "All this mess we are in is the fault of the Communists!" Now it is true that the Communists have become involved in the world revolution and are taking advantage of it, but they did not initiate it. It is really the Christians who sparked the present revolution. Messengers of Christ went everywhere preaching the love of God and dignity of the human person. They told people, "God loves everybody—rich and poor, educated and uneducated, black and white, European and Asian. Christ died on the cross for the whole world—for Indians, Africans, Chinese, Koreans, Japanese, Americans, Italians, Brazilians, Mexicans, English, French—all people! Every person, regardless of race, color, or class, is of value to God and can become a son or daughter of God." Christian missionaries backed up these words with noble deeds. They ministered to the sick, poor, illiterate, outcast, and oppressed. They started schools, hospitals, orphanages, leprosariums, and homes for widows and the aged. The amazing ideas that they proclaimed and the loving service they performed became the sparks that lit the revolution of rising expectations and human dignity among the common people of the world.

Actually, the United States as a nation contributed a great deal to the revolution. We were the first to give the idea of a real democracy to the rest of the world. We said all people were created equal and had certain inalienable rights given to them by God Himself—freedom, opportunity, and justice. For many years the colonized and suppressed nations looked to America as their model and hero. Of course, we did not always live up to our ideals and beliefs, and our failures finally caught up with us in the 1960s with the civil rights movement. We have made much progress, though we still have a long way to go. But even today America is looked upon as the land of freedom and opportunity by countless millions around the world.

Where do the Communists come into the picture? We already said that this world revolution is not essentially a Communist revolution, and this is true. But we must also realize that the great human revolt and the two ideas that sparked it have been cleverly *used* by the Communists for their own purposes. They have stepped into the situation and have often taken over, or tried to take over, the revolt. They have tried to identify the movement as their own, pervert it, and channel it for their own selfish ends. How often we have seen the Russians taking the side of a guerrilla movement in some country, on pretense of an interest in freedom, only to find that the new government has become a puppet in Communist hands, as in Afghanistan, Mozambique, Angola, and Ethiopia. However, instead of blaming the Communists for everything that happens, we should be sure that our own house is in order. We need to take our stand for freedom and justice wherever they are in peril. With that in mind, let us note some of the major political aspects of the world revolution and ways in which they affect the world mission of the church.

The Death of Colonialism
Right after World War II we began to witness the breakup of Western colonial empires. Between 1946 and 1957, most of the Asian countries gained independence, including the Philippines, India, Burma, Pakistan, Sri Lanka, Indonesia, and Malaysia. These nations comprised over 600 million people at the time. Shortly afterward, the French were forced to pull out of French Indochina, including present-day Vietnam, Laos, and Cambodia. From Asia the freedom movement leaped over to Africa, and in the early 1960s, twenty-one new nations were born on that continent. A few small pockets of colonialism are left in the world, but they will soon disappear. Colonialism is now a thing of the past. We do not lament this fact, for freedom is the birthright of every people. Political independence has brought new life, hope, and impetus to all the new nations.

The Rise of Nationalism
Along with political independence has come a new surge of nationalism throughout the Afro-Asian countries. It is expressed in a spirit of national pride, patriotism, and a desire to be free from all outside interference. Nationalism has brought both problems and benefits to the church and Christian missions.

The end of colonialism means that the Christian enterprise is now having to move against the tide, not with it. Previously missions had the protection of the strong arm of colonial governments, which were at least nominally Christian and sympathetic to missions. It was easy for missionaries to obtain visas to enter a country and to get permission to open new work. They had a free hand to evangelize. Today's missionaries are guests in the host country and therefore have no rights, only privileges. They no longer enjoy prestige and special concessions. Respect is not automatically granted; it has to be earned. Many governments, such as those in China, North Korea, Vietnam, Burma, Iraq, Iran, Libya, and Algeria, have forced missionaries to leave the country. Some governments, such as those of India, Malaysia, and Indonesia, restrict the entry of missionaries, while others, as in Nepal, restrict the activity of missionaries to purely humanitarian services. Missionaries are still needed in many of these lands, but we should not let the situation drive us to despair. We can be encouraged by the history of Christian missions. In many instances missionaries who were forced to leave a country later returned to find that the church had grown tremendously in their absence in spite of persecution. Furthermore, we are finding today that lay Christian witnesses are able to enter many doors that have been closed to the professional missionary. More will be said about this in a later chapter.

Colonialism and Christianity have been linked together in the minds of the Afro-Asian people, since colonialism and the modern Protestant missionary movement developed during the same period in history. Sometimes the missionary followed in the steps of the colonist; at other times the colonist entered the scene after the missionary. This does not mean that the two worked arm in arm or that they had the same goals and strategy. In the beginning, East India companies were very antagonistic to the entrance and work of missionaries. On the other side, missionaries were often the only ones who championed the rights of the local people and spoke out against injustices of the colonists. But since missionary and colonist were both from the West and came at about the same time, in the minds of many Africans and Asians missionary and colonist were linked together. Many felt that the Christian church was the right arm of imperialism. The result of this mentality has been that in turning against colonialism, many people in the East have also turned against Christianity, the "religion of the imperialist."

In time, however, this problem may solve itself, for today at least one generation of young people, born in the postindependence era, have never known the days of colonialism. Furthermore, even after all colonial administrators pulled out of these countries, Christian missionaries stayed on and continued to minister in love to human needs. Thus, the linkage between colonialism and Christianity is slowly being erased from the minds of the people of Africa and Asia.

Nationalism has resulted in a rediscovery of national cultures and histories. In the days of colonialism there was a certain aura about "Western civilization" in the eyes of many non-Westerners. They wanted to mimic the ways of their foreign rulers. Now Africans and Asians realize there are vices as well as virtues in European culture, and they want to be free to reject customs and lifestyles that are harmful to their societies and accept those that are beneficial. At the same time they want to retain values of their own cultures and the right to be themselves.

One symbol of this spirit of nationalism is the way in which some governments have removed old statues and monuments of former viceroys, kings, and queens, and replaced them with statues of national heroes. They have also gone back to indigenous names for their countries and cities. Ceylon was changed to Sri Lanka; the Belgian Congo to Zaire; Southern Rhodesia to Zimbabwe. In Zaire, Leopoldville became Kinshasa; Stanleyville, Kisangani; and Elisabethville, Lubumbashi. In India, South Parade was changed to Mahatma Gandhi Road, and Hornby to Dadabhai Naoroji Road.

People living in countries that were once colonies are very sensitive to any criticism of their culture and society, especially from the West. They don't mind criticizing the West, at times quite harshly, but at the same time they resent criticism of themselves. Sometimes these people may appear to us to be overly sensitive, but we have to understand the reason for this. Asians are still not sure whether our criticism is sincere or just an expression of our feeling of superiority— a holdover from colonial days. They are not sure whether we are honestly trying to help or are just making fun of them.

Perhaps in time the people of Africa and Asia will become more mature in this regard, but they are still in the infancy of their independence and seek to jealously guard their freedom and self-image. Anyway, we must be very careful of referring to them as "natives," "pagans," "uncivilized," or "underdeveloped." After all, in a country like India, for example, the people are far more "religious" than many Americans, and their civilization is hundreds of years older than ours.

Nationalism is also throwing into bold relief the "foreignness" of Christianity. People get the impression that to become a Christian is to forsake one's own cultural heritage and adopt a foreign culture. Christianity is looked upon as a subtle form of "religious imperialism," which robs people of their national distinctiveness. This is all the more reason that missionaries today must be careful not to transplant a Western form of Christianity to other countries, but rather allow the seed of the Gospel to grow in the cultural soil of the land. This is more fully discussed in a later chapter.

Political independence has also produced a new spirit of independence in the church. Whenever an African or Asian nation gained its independence, it immediately became embarrassed to have an institution within its borders, namely the church, that was being run by foreigners. People began to say among themselves, "If we have persons intelligent enough to be prime minister, president, finance minister, minister of foreign affairs, governor, and others, surely we have persons who are capable of being moderator, bishop, superintendent, or treasurer of the church." And so the development of national leadership for the church became a high priority. Some mission boards had already done a good job in this area, but others were slow to turn over the reins of administration to their converts. The prevailing spirit of nationalism served as a strong impetus to speed up the process of leadership training.

Today, churches across the seas, except those in certain pioneering areas, are all self-governing, and many have chosen to be autonomous from their founding denominational bodies in the West. They still maintain affiliation with the home church and continue to receive financial support and personnel from abroad, but they are governed by their own synods and general conferences and make their own decisions. Many churches in Asia and Africa have gone together to form their own unions, so we find the United Church of the Philippines, the United Church of Japan (the Kyodan), the United Church of Pakistan, the Church of South India, the Church of North India, the United Church of Zaire, and so on. In all of these developments we can certainly rejoice.

The Threat of Communism
While millions have gained their political freedom since World War II, other millions have lost their freedom. In the last few decades the countries of over a billion people have changed their political affiliation. While Western imperialism has all but died out, an imperialism of a far more sinister nature has taken over. As we already pointed out, Communism did not originate the present "revolution" that is sweeping the world, but it does take advantage of it and seeks to direct it to its own ends. It especially makes use of poverty, social injustice, Western imperialism, or racial prejudice to get a foothold in a particular country. Thus, we find Marxist revolutionary governments in Angola, Mozambique, Congo (Brazzaville), Ethiopia, China, Cuba, Vietnam, and North Korea. We will need to keep our eyes on South Africa these days, for the Communists are sure to take advantage of the tragic policy of apartheid and the political unrest it fosters in order to establish themselves in that strategic area of the world.

Communism makes a special appeal to the masses by the promises it makes. Its leaders say to the people: "We know the government is trying to do something for you, but the wheels of democracy move very slowly. It may take twenty-five to thirty years before they can improve your lot. How long can you afford to wait? Put us in power and we'll change things overnight!" It doesn't matter whether the Communists are able to fulfill their promises or not; the promises sound good.

Christians must make themselves familiar with the beliefs, organization, and methods of the Communists. We need to be acquainted with the charges brought by Communism against Christianity and be prepared to deal with them. We should know the main ideas of Communism and have intelligent answers to them.

However, we Christians must be careful that we don't develop a phobia regarding Communism, nor seek to use the threat of Communism as a motive for Christian missions. How often we have heard something like this: "Communism is threatening to engulf the continents of Africa and Asia. Christianity is the only antidote to Communism. Therefore, we must get the Gospel to these lands before Communism takes over. The choice is Christianity or Communism. We must move fast."

Now, it is true that Communism *is* a serious threat and that genuine Christianity *is* an antidote to Communism. But to use the Gospel merely as a tool to fight off Communism is to miss the whole point of Christian missions. Our purpose is not to fight Communism; it is to proclaim the good news of Jesus Christ. To say that we are for missions because they fight Communism is to manipulate the Gospel for our own ends. We do not use the Gospel *against* Communism, or for that matter, against Buddhism, Hinduism, Islam, secularism, or any other "ism." We witness to the saving and liberating power of Christ and reject anything that falls short of the fullness of Christ.

Though we reject Marxist philosophy and strategy, we must learn from the Communist movement and seek to define and practice the Christian alternative to Communism. Communism is challenging the Christian church in several different areas.

It is challenging the church to a proper social application of the Gospel. Communists have achieved much success by posing as the champions of the poor and the oppressed. Christians have often suffered loss by appearing to uphold the status quo. Certainly no one should be more concerned about the poor and the suffering than the followers of the compassionate Saviour. As Christians we must minister to the needy and cry out against all forms of injustice—social, economic, and political.

Communism is challenging the church to simplified and consecrated living. Someone has said that a false idea supported by zealous and dedicated people can win over a true idea whose followers sit idly by and do nothing. Communists often boast that they live a simple life and are willing to sacrifice anything to achieve their goals. Christians must outdo the Communists in heroism, devotion, and simplicity of living. It was said of the early Christians that they outthought, outlived, and out-died their critics and adversaries. In our day the same must be true of representatives of the Gospel as contrasted with the followers of Marx.

Communists are challenging the church to distinguish between the essential Gospel and its cultural wrappings. One of the main pieces of propaganda that Communists use to deter people from accepting the Christian faith is: "Christianity is a foreign religion. It is the white man's religion." As Christians we must make it plain that we are not exporting Western culture or the American way of life (they can pick that to pieces), but we are bringing the liberating news of the Saviour, Jesus Christ (and no one can find fault in Him). We must point out that Christ was born in the Middle East, and the Gospel was brought to Europe by Asian missionaries.

A young lad in Africa asked a missionary, "What color skin did Jesus have? Was He white like you, or black like me?" The missionary answered, "He was neither white nor black, but somewhat in between, a tan or brown color."

The boy thought for a while, then smiled and said, "That's good! It means that Jesus belongs to both of us." Indeed, He belongs to people of all colors and races and cultures. He is the universal Christ.

Finally, the Communists are challenging us to produce and distribute good literature. It has often been said that the Christians teach people to read, but the Communists supply literature for them to read. The Soviet government spends billions of dollars each year on literature for export to Asia, Africa, and Latin America. Most of the publications contain subtle propaganda for Marxism. I remember seeing a small booklet in India entitled, "Thirty Ways to Prepare Rice." It was a very simple but helpful book for village women. On the last page was written: "Published by the Communist Party of India. Now you know who cares for you. The next time you go to the polls, vote for the hammer and sickle." We Christians need to produce all kinds of good literature, not just for political propaganda, but for the minds and hearts of people and their general welfare.

Political Unrest

Many Afro-Asian countries have obtained their independence and have withstood the inroads of Communism, but at the same time have fallen prey to revolutionary governments of their own. Of the 158 nations in the world today, only about 40 enjoy complete freedom, 53 are partially free, and 65 have few if any civil rights. Kingdoms rise and fall. Of 47 independent states in Africa, 43 are controlled by dictatorships, military rule, one-party rule, or a president for life.

Missionaries these days have to walk the tightrope. They can no longer feel secure or count on spending their whole careers in one area. Today's government may be friendly and missionaries allowed to work in peace, but tomorrow's government may be hostile and order them to leave. Missionaries have been caught in the cross fires of civil war in Angola, Burundi, Zaire, and Vietnam, and several of them have been brutally murdered by guerrilla bands. In some places, missionaries have been kidnapped and held for ransom. The news of the shooting of Chet Bitterman, Wycliffe missionary in Colombia, South America, is still fresh in our minds. Christians at home base certainly need to pray constantly for the safety and physical welfare of their representatives on the front lines.

EIGHT

OUR RELIGIOUS AND SOCIOECONOMIC WORLD

Not long ago a Christian missionary in Sri Lanka (formerly Ceylon) received a visit from a Buddhist priest who wanted to borrow some books on Christianity. "I didn't know you were interested in Christianity," said the missionary.

"I am not," was the reply, "but my job is to train young monks who will go as missionaries to the West; and I think it's a good idea that they should know something of the religion of the natives before they get there."

We may smile at this story, but it should cause us to pause and reflect, for it is indicative of the religious climate of our day. It is symbolic of many changes that have taken place in the last several years. The Christian messenger of today is living in a vastly different world from that of his predecessors.

The Religious World of Today

A few decades ago the non-Christian religions appeared to be on the decline. They were dormant, silent, on the defensive, more or less accepting the superiority of the Christian faith. But now with the coming of independence to Afro-Asian nations, the people have been reaching back into their own history, culture, and indigenous religious faith. They have sought new religious foundations to help build up their political systems and maintain national unity. Opposition to the political, cultural, and religious domination of the West during the days of colonialism has led Asians to return to the "faith of their fathers" with renewed zeal. This has resulted in a "revival" of the world religions, particularly Buddhism, Islam, and Hinduism. Believers in these religions are on the march today. They are vocal, aggressive, and quick to claim universal validity for their religions. They are copying many methods employed by the Christian church and are carrying on their own missionary programs.

Signs of religious revival can be seen all across the world these days. A few years ago I was in Penang, Malaysia. Walking down a main street, I saw a large imposing building with the sign: Y.M.B.A. Now I know what the Y.M.C.A. is, but I was curious about the Y.M.B.A. When I asked someone on the street, he told me that Y.M.B.A. stood for the "Young Men's Buddhist Association." I went into the building and found the front room was the worship center, where people were kneeling and praying to a large image of Buddha. Beyond that was the Buddhist Sunday School—that is what they called it—and I heard children singing some familiar tunes, but with a few changes in the words. They sang, "Buddha, lover of my soul," and "Buddha loves me this I know, for the Dhamma tells me so." (The Dhamma is the Buddhist religious system.) I found that the chief priest was an American, the former Dr. Robert Clifton, with a Ph.D. in chemical engineering. He had been converted to Buddhism in Japan and then appointed to service in Penang. He had taken the name of The Venerable Sumangala. Because of his Christian background, he used many Christian terms in his conversation with me, and spoke of Buddha as "the Word become flesh." Suddenly I realized that I was up against a new Buddhism.

While preaching in Colombo, capital city of Sri Lanka, I saw posters on the street asking for contributions "for the spread of the Gospel of Buddha to the pagan of Europe." I visited a Buddhist seminary in the city where they are training Buddhist monks in Hindi and English in preparation for missionary service in India and the English-speaking world.

Islam is also on the march today. One aggressive Muslim sect has its mission headquarters in Rabwah, Pakistan, whence they have sent forth several hundred foreign missionaries into various countries of the world. This group produces a mass of literature that seeks to confute the basic truths of the Christian faith. They claim that Jesus did not die on the cross, that He escaped and fled to Kashmir, where He died and was buried in Shrinagar. A Muslim missionary in Lagos, Nigeria challenged Billy Graham to a public religious debate when the latter was conducting a campaign in that country a few years ago. Then when Billy Graham went on to Nairobi, Kenya, a Muslim missionary challenged him to a public healing service. "Let us take thirty incurable patients," he proposed, "and by lot you take fifteen and I'll take fifteen. Let us see who can heal the most!"

In Cairo, Egypt, the Supreme Islamic Council carries on an aggressive missionary program for the continent of Africa. Training camps are turning out scores of lay missionaries in a concerted effort to win the uncommitted animist tribes in central and southern Africa. Printing presses flood the continent with cheap copies of the Koran and pamphlets that proclaim the word of Allah. In Libya, a tax-supported Islamic center with a $20-million budget is directing propagation of the Muslim faith in thirty-five other countries.

A main characteristic of the religious revival movement has been the tendency toward establishing state religions, that is, making the religion of the majority the national religion. In Burma, for example, for several years Buddhism was declared to be the state religion. In Afghanistan, Pakistan, and the Middle East, Islam is considered to be the state religion. India has succeeded so far in maintaining freedom of religion and separation of state and religion, but there is an aggressive segment of Hindu society that would like to see "India for the Hindus." In each case the majority religion is equated with patriotism—"To be a loyal Burmese, you must be Buddhist; to be a genuine Pakistani, you must be Muslim"—and the loyalty of those in minority groups is questioned.

Iran is probably the outstanding illustration of religion taking over the state. The reins of government have passed from king to priest; Islam is clearly the state religion, and Islamic law is the rule of the land. Leadership is seeking to establish a theocratic government based on the will of Allah and is attempting to spread Islamic revolution throughout the Middle East.

As a direct result of this religious revival around the world, the Christian faith is being challenged to a greater extent than ever before. Today non-Christians are highly critical of Christians in the West and seem to delight in pointing out our failure to live up to our own standards. They remind us of our high divorce rate, ever-increasing crime rate, our obsession with free sex, two world wars that originated in "Christian Europe," and our involvement with the arms race. Many non-Christians are also contesting the right of Christians to convert others to their faith. They argue that conversion muddles the convert's sense of unity and solidarity with his society, so there is danger of his loyalty to country and state being undermined. Still others are challenging the Christian claim to uniqueness and final truth. They suggest that no religion possesses the whole truth, and that all religions are on an equal footing. So we ought to quit arguing about who is right and who is wrong and join in a common search for truth. Christians should seek to make better Christians; Hindus, better Hindus; Muslims, better Muslims; Buddhists, better Buddhists. We all should accept the validity of one another's religions, and join in the common battle against secularism and atheism.

Christians must face all these challenges squarely and honestly. In response to criticisms of our behavior, we dare not attempt to cover up or rationalize our failures. We must sincerely confess our sins before God and our fellowmen, come to the Heavenly Father in genuine repentance and humility, ask for full and free forgiveness, and then by the grace of God try to live out the Christian life in love and holiness. Non-Christians must see that to be a Christian is to be different from the world and to be like Christ in motive, attitude, word, and deed. We must take our stand against the moral evils and injustices of our day and seek to change not only individuals but society as well. We must try to strengthen the foundations of family life and to renew the spiritual life of the church. Nominal Christians must become genuine Christians.

In response to the challenge against the biblical claim to

ultimate truth and the call for spiritual conversion, evangelical Christians must unashamedly declare that these matters are nonnegotiable. The uniqueness of Christ is not something that we claim for Christ, but something that He claimed for Himself. He said clearly, "I am the way, and the truth, and the life; no one comes to the Father, but by Me" (John 14:6). He claimed to be "the light of the world" and the source of eternal life (John 8:12; 11:25). He claimed to be the "Son of God" (John 10:36; 5:17-18), to have authority to forgive sins (Matt. 9:1-8), and to judge the world (John 5:22-25). These are fantastic claims. No other man—not even Buddha or Mohammed—made such amazing statements about himself. The claim that Jesus is the only Saviour is not merely something we concede to Christ, but something with which He *confronts us.*

The Social and Economic World of Today

Once independence had been achieved, the new nations turned their attention to the struggle to build their nations. Gaining freedom was relatively easy in most cases, but to retain it has proved difficult. There are internal divisions, lack of trained personnel, corruption in government, and widespread disillusionment. But the gains outweigh the losses. Asia and Africa are going through birth pangs of independence, making mistakes, but learning. There is a sense of responsibility for uplifting the masses.

Significant changes have taken place in Afro-Asian societies in the past few decades. For one thing, the status of women has greatly improved. In many countries, for a long time women were little better than servants. Now they have been given the right to vote; they have become a political entity. There is a move in some Muslim countries to do away with the practice of women wearing veils to cover their faces in public. In India the Hindu Code Bill has provided for monogamy, rights of divorce, and the right of inheritance for women. Education for women has steadily developed. They are entering many new positions of public service, such as nurses, teachers, secretaries, telephone operators, bus conductors, and airline flight attendants. Several have entered the field of medicine; some have gone into politics. A few years ago in Sri Lanka, Mrs. Bandaranaike was elected for one term as prime minister upon the assassination of her husband who had held that office. The first governor of the United Provinces in India was a woman, Mrs. Naidu. The first Indian ambassador to the United States was Mrs. Pandit, who for a time was president of the General Assembly in the United Nations. Another woman, Rajkumari Amrit Kaur, was the first minister of health in Pandit Nehru's cabinet. More recently, Mrs. Indira Gandhi was prime minister of India for three terms. Now, Mrs. Aquino is president of the Philippines.

Great strides have been made in the field of education. Up until the time of political independence, most schools in Africa and Asia were run by the Christian church (85 percent in Africa). Eastern countries now realize that unless their people become literate and possess a fair degree of education, all attempts at social reform will end in failure, and they will not take their rightful places in the community of nations. In the past, education was the privilege of a few; now it is becoming a possibility for all. Most governments consider elementary education the first charge on state resources, and they are making primary education compulsory for all youth. It is a big task. There are so many pupils and so few trained teachers and adequate buildings. But these days one can see many new grade schools being opened in rural areas, and a good number of colleges and universities in cities. When Zaire gained its independence from Belgium in 1960, there was only one university in the whole country—it was three years old and run by the Catholic Church—and there were only about ten college graduates. Today there are three major universities in Zaire with over 25,000 students enrolled, and several other affiliated colleges.

Progress has been made in other areas as well, but we do not have space to discuss all these matters. We will, however, note three important aspects of the present socioeconomic environment that are influencing the worldwide mission of the church.

The Population Explosion
One of the basic problems facing the world today, and particularly the Afro-Asian countries, is rapid population

growth. Experts tell us that in the days of Jesus the world population was possibly only about 300 million. It was not until the year 1650 that it had doubled to become 600 million. Only in the year 1830 did the world population for the first time reach the 1-billion mark. By 1930 it was 2 billion, in 1965, 3 billion; in 1980, 4 billion. In 1987 it stood at roughly 5 billion. If the population continues to increase at this rate, it will be over 6 billion by the end of the century.

The population of most Asian countries has doubled since they gained their independence. In 1947 India had 350 million people; today it has 750 million, growing at the rate of 14 million a year. Since the Communists took over mainland China in 1949, the population has grown from 560 million to slightly over 1 billion. Bangladesh, which is just the size of the state of Wisconsin, has a population of over 90 million. If the population destiny of the United States were as high as that of Bangladesh, we would contain the entire world population of 5 billion within our borders.

Two significant factors arise from the population explosion. First is the economic problem. Imagine how many more mouths there are to be fed each year; how many more schools and houses have to be constructed; how many more jobs are needed. The Afro-Asian nations are making progress in industry and agriculture, but most of the gains are swallowed up in the numbers game.

For a number of years India has been carrying on strong propaganda for family planning and birth control. Slogans can be seen everywhere on streets and walls of buildings. However, cultural and economic factors hinder the attempt to keep the population down. People prefer large families, for this is the "social security system" of the land. Sons are expected to take care of their parents when they get old, so the more sons one has, the more secure one will be after retirement. As for rural people, they either do not see the value of family planning or do not have money to buy contraceptives, so they continue to have large families.

China has taken drastic steps in recent years to bring its population growth under control. It officially advocates one child per family and imposes severe economic burdens on families that have a second or third child. This is causing

many problems in Chinese society today. Children are growing up alone with no brothers or sisters, and in a few years
there will be no uncles or aunts. Abortion is being practiced
widely in cases of second pregnancies. But the government is
determined to do something about overpopulation.

From a spiritual standpoint, the world population explosion poses a tremendous challenge for the Christian church.
It means that there are simply more people to be reached
and won for Christ than ever before in the history of the
church. It means that the propagation of the Gospel of divine
grace is not keeping pace with the procreation of the human
race; the birthrate of the kingdom of God is not keeping pace
with the birthrate of the kingdom of mankind.

To God all this is more than mere statistics. To Him earth's
population is not just a mass of humanity, but is composed of
persons—men, women, boys, and girls—for whom Christ
died. The greatest desire in the heart of the Father is the
salvation of the people of the world. Each individual is
precious to Him and is known to Him by name.

Once a minister was visiting a family of his congregation.
He noticed many children in the home, so he asked the
mother, "How many children do you have?"

She began to count them off on her fingers, "John, Lucy,
Mary, David—" when the minister interrupted, "I don't want
their names—I asked for the number."

The mother replied indignantly, "They have names, not
numbers!"

So also in God's sight, the teeming millions of the world
are not just a mass of numbers, but are precious persons
whom God knows by name and by need. The growing population of the world presents us with the greatest task of the
age. The harvest is getting larger and larger all the time.
These are not days for retrenchment, but for advance. We
need more laborers than ever before.

Growth of the Cities

In the last few decades the entire world has witnessed a great
rush to the cities. People from villages and rural areas are
migrating at the rate of 27 million a year to cities, seeking
jobs, education, and a more exciting lifestyle. As a result,

cities everywhere are overcrowded. Over 200 cities around the world have populations of 1 million or more. Mexico City is presently the world's largest, with over 18 million people; the number is expected to swell to 26 million by the year 2000. Sao Paulo, Brazil (now 13 million) is due to grow to 24 million by the same date. Tokyo (12 million) will reach 17 million; greater New York, 15.5 million; Calcutta and Bombay, India (now 9 million) will pass the 16-million mark. In the year 2000 there will be 35 cities with over 7 million people each, and 78 with over 4 million; more than half the world's people will live in large cities.

The chaos arising from this rush to urban centers is readily apparent. Providing basic public services that urban life demands—sewage, garbage disposal, water, electricity, housing, and transportation—is proving to be a major problem. Even New York City nearly went bankrupt in 1975. When millions of people are pressed together—many of them poor, uneducated, and unemployed—the crime rate soars, quality of education diminishes, and demand for public services of all kinds increases.

To see how dire conditions in a city can become, one only needs to visit Calcutta in northeast India. Calcutta is so lost in everything big, crowded, and old that its misery defies human description. Calcutta's 9 million people are packed 90,000 to the square mile. It is estimated that 80 percent of the families live in single rooms. This leaves 200,000 people for whom the pavement is the only home they know. As many as thirty persons share a single water tap, and twenty a single latrine. A fourth of Calcutta's food supply is consumed by rats. Some 40 percent of the students at Calcutta University, which has an enrollment of over 100,000, suffer from malnutrition. Major diseases are rampant. Suffering is beyond imagination.

The social and economic problems of today's great cities are apparent to everyone. But there is a far greater problem of a different kind, which is the central concern of Christians. It is the spiritual condition of city people. In many cities across the world, Christian churches have pulled out of the downtown areas and fled to the suburbs, allowing the heart of the city to become a cesspool of crime and vice. This is tragic. We have to tackle the citadels of evil afresh.

In years past, Christian missions have definitely concentrated on rural areas. This was proper at the time, for the majority of people lived in villages and small towns. But the situation is different now. Concentrations of people are in the cities. Furthermore, it is in the cities that political and economic power resides and where major decisions affecting the nation are made. Cities set the pace for society. All the fads, fashions, and new lifestyles originate in the city and then spread out to the countryside. As spokes in a wheel lead to the hub, so all roads lead to urban centers. Cultural centers, skyscrapers, mass media for communication, and the majority of leaders are all in the city. The church around the world will now have to become more urban oriented in its thinking and planning if it is to win the world for Christ. Many Christians still have the idea that missions means working among "savages" living in mud huts in a jungle somewhere. But they forget the tens of thousands of "pagans" who reside in modern apartments in cement jungles.

South Korea and some republics of Latin America are the only areas where the church is making a serious impact on urban centers. Seoul, capital of South Korea, now has over 4,000 churches within its boundaries, and this number is increasing every year. In Sao Paulo, Brazil and Santiago, Chile may be found many large evangelical congregations with spacious church buildings that accommodate thousands of worshipers in a single service. Pentecostal groups are doing an excellent job of winning poor, rural people who are migrating from *pueblos* into the cities, looking for jobs and a better way of life. These people get lost in the city but find the friendship and hope that they need in the fellowship of Pentecostal believers.

Cities of the world are waiting to be stormed by God's faithful servants. They are places of challenges and opportunity. They are strategic centers of conflict that need to be won for Christ.

Hunger and Poverty

Senator Mark Hatfield has reminded us that "the greatest threat to this nation and the stability of the entire world is hunger. It is more explosive than all the atomic weaponry possessed by the big powers. Desperate people do desperate things" ("World Hunger," *World Vision,* February 1975, p. 5).

Famine, malnutrition, hunger, and starvation—these are specters that stalk many parts of the world today. In recent months what could easily be the worst famine of the twentieth century has been devastating twenty-four African countries—an area twice the size of the United States. Hundreds of thousands have died, and millions will suffer in health in the years to come. The United Nations estimates that between ten and fifteen thousand people around the world die every day from malnutrition or starvation. One billion people have stunted bodies or damaged brains because of inadequate food.

Population growth is not the principal cause of our present world crisis; it is largely a symptom. The basic cause is poverty. The fact is that in virtually every country where poverty has been corrected (such as Taiwan and Singapore), there has been an immediate and dramatic drop in population growth. When the standard of living is raised, people don't feel the need to have as many children to provide for their security in old age. It is very naive for the people in the Western world to demand that "the backward nations stop producing more babies and start producing more food." It is certainly important to help the poor in family planning, but it is even more vital to aggressively attack the primary cause of population growth—poverty.

A common myth is that we don't have enough food in the world for everyone. The fact is we *do* have enough food right now to adequately meet the needs of every man, woman, and child. *Imbalance* in food distribution is the number one reason a hunger problems stalks our world today. People with money can always buy food; famine affects only the poor. When food scarcity causes an increase in the price of grain imports, middle- and upper-income persons in developing countries continue to eat. But millions of people who are already devoting 60 to 80 percent of their incomes to food simply eat less and die sooner. Death is usually the result of a disease that underfed bodies cannot resist.

In spite of much progress made in recent years in the fields of agriculture and industry, there is an ever-widening gap between the standards of living found in developed and developing countries. For example, in the United States the annual per capita income is around $9,000; in one half of the world it is less than $200. Life expectancy in the United States is 73 years; in most developing countries it averages about 55. Whereas Americans spend 17 percent of their income on food, in India they spend 67 percent. While there is one doctor to every 600 persons in the United States, there is only one per 11,000 in Haiti.

The sad fact is that the high standard of living in the developed nations is largely at the expense of the poor nations of the world. We Americans are only 6 percent of the world's population, but we consume 40 percent of the world's resources. If all the world's people tried to live under the current standard of a North American, only 18 percent could remain alive; the other 82 percent would die because of lack of resources. Much of America's resources come from other countries, including poor nations. One of our favorite hamburger chains raises its beef on scarce fertile land in Haiti, the poorest nation in the Western Hemisphere, where 25 percent of the children are undernourished. As we in the United States put millions of acres of our best agricultural land under shopping centers and parking lots, we are increasingly turning to the Southern Hemisphere for many of our agricultural products. Rich nations import twice as many dollars worth of food from poor nations as they export to them.

Someone asks, "Are we not giving a lot of aid to these other countries?" Not really, when we consider how much we spend on ourselves. America has a national budget of $221 billion to defend itself from other nations. It has a foreign aid budget of $4.2 billion to help those nations. The United States did display national generosity at the end of World War II. At the height of the Marshall Plan (begun in 1947 to rebuild war-torn Europe), we actually gave annually 2.79 percent of our gross national product for development assistance. But by 1975 that figure had plummeted to a mere 0.24 percent of the GNP, but our total GNP had doubled!

The United States actually ranks fifth from the bottom (in percentage of GNP given) among the seventeen major Western donors of foreign aid.

The people of America have not been blind nor insensitive to the problems of hunger and poverty. Private aid to overseas needs (including giving to missions) amounts to approximately $2 billion a year. Christians in particular have been at the forefront of relief aid through such outstanding agencies as World Vision, World Relief, United Methodist Committee on Overseas Relief, Compassion, Food for the Hungry, and a host of others. Christians have demonstrated their compassion for suffering millions at times of great national calamities, such as the Sahel famine in Africa, the earthquake in Mexico, and the mud slide in Colombia, South America. But Christians have also come to realize that private efforts to assist hungry people are not enough; we need to influence government policies which can either multiply or nullify all the private efforts. Bread for the World, the Christian antihunger lobbying group in Washington, D.C., won a long-sought victory in the latter part of the Carter administration when Congress voted the establishment of an emergency grain reserve. The government-owned reserve, containing 4 million tons of wheat, is being used to alleviate famines and other extreme food shortages around the world.

One very significant lesson we learned from recent decades of wrestling with problems of poverty and calamity is that charity alone is not enough. It is merely a temporary patch that doesn't really get to the heart of the problem. Furthermore, a handout only produces a deadly dependency and leaves people where they are. We have shown this in Haiti and elsewhere. What people need is not just a handout, but a helping hand that will enable them to stand on their own feet and regain their dignity. The old Chinese proverb stills makes good sense: "Give a man a fish, and he will have a meal; teach him how to fish, and he will have a living."

Relief agencies are giving more and more attention to development projects. They are providing necessary skills and land and capital for people to produce their own food and goods. By giving hoes instead of handouts to farmers made destitute by war and typhoon, World Relief enabled more than 12,000 families in Bangladesh to not only care for themselves but market their produce at home and abroad. By giving seeds instead of rice to refugee farmers in Cambodia, World Vision was able to convince the people that they themselves could overcome their tragic circumstances and make their world over again. In many parts of the world where the development of water resources is essential, Christian organizations have helped communities dig tube wells. Those wells not only help agriculture; it is estimated that they will reduce communicable diseases in villages by as much as 60 percent. In Bangladesh, a Christian organization (HEED) trained Lal, a local young man, to make baskets and furniture out of wild bamboo and cane, which grow profusely in the area. Now Lal runs a training center. But not only did Lal learn to support himself and help others, he also became a Christian. Today, in his spare time, he conducts literacy classes on his own for his people.

Dr. Anthony Campolo, sociology professor at Eastern College and former missionary to the Dominican Republic, along with a few friends, bought some shares of stock in the multinational corporation Gulf and Western. They attended the stockholders' meetings and confronted executives and major shareholders with allegations of exploitation in the Dominican Republic. At the suggestion of the Christian group, Gulf and Western committed itself to investing in an agricultural college and soon after allocated $100 million for the social and economic benefit of the Republic. Even corporations can be influenced.

Space does not permit the narration of all the exciting projects being undertaken by various Christian organizations across the world. If the reader is interested in pursuing the subject, we highly recommend the book *God's Foreign Policy: Practical Ways to Help the World's Poor,* by Miriam Adeney. It is both informing and inspiring.

One thing is certain. If the Gospel is going to appear relevant and meaningful to millions of destitute people across the world, we as Christians must demonstrate that we not only love to proclaim the good news of salvation, but we also love people and desire to help them in all of their needs. The Christian voice for righteousness, justice, and a fair chance for all must not be silent amidst the selfish shouts of Marxist or capitalist extremes. We must wage the war against hunger and poverty on two fronts: helping people help themselves within their own environment and standing without retreat against oppressive forces that enslave the poor.

NINE

THE MISSIONARY'S ROLE TODAY

The birth of political independence and the maturing of the church in Afro-Asian countries have produced a change in role (or function) for the foreign missionary. This role has gone through four distinct stages.

The role of the pioneer. This was the first period before a church had been established on a particular field. The area was "virgin territory" to be evangelized. Churches from abroad, in obedience to the command of Christ, sent their messengers to proclaim the Gospel to those who had never heard before. Early missionaries were thus pioneers who had the field to themselves. They had enormous physical difficulties, dangers, and hardships; but spiritually they were free. Their only limits were the bounds of their own energy and talents. They were on their own and could do as they pleased, without having to consult anyone from the outside. This was the day of the rugged individualist. Missionaries like William Carey, David Livingstone, Hudson Taylor, and Mary Slessor are good examples of such pioneers.

The role of administrator. This stage naturally followed the pioneer phase. When converts were received and incorporated into the church of Christ, the next step was to organize, instruct, and supervise these visible congregations. Institutions such as schools and hospitals were founded and needed to be managed. Since indigenous leadership had not yet been developed, missionaries assumed these responsibil-

105

ities. The missionary gradually changed from pioneer to administrator.

The role of specialist. As national Christians received training and experience in various fields, many administrative posts were handed over from missionaries to nationals. This, of course, was all to the good and was the very aim of the mission society from the beginning. Then the missionary became more or less a specialist in some area of the work, such as nursing tutor, teacher trainer, seminary professor, or evangelism demonstrator. This permitted the missionary to become a pioneer once again, not in the geographical sense of entering new territory, but in the area of new ideas and methods. New opportunities developed for pioneering in such areas as race relations, preventive medicine, education, various forms of research, new methods of evangelism, and audiovisual aids. The spiritual opportunities in these areas were and are enormous for the right kind of specialist with the right spiritual qualities.

The role of servant. Now it seems clear that the missionary is entering a fourth stage, taking on the role of coworker or partner. Missionaries will not have the status of important church positions nor a dominant voice in public. Missionaries will have to depend more and more on their own moral and spiritual influence and authority and will have to be experts in right relationships. To use an illustration from basketball, the missionary will be more of a guard than a center or forward, but will still be on the team and in the game.

All during this time the attitude of nationals toward the missionary has also undergone some changes. Perhaps this can best be described in the words of a national, Dr. S.P. Adirayan of India:

> The attitude of the Indian Christian toward the missionary has, during the last one hundred years, gone through three stages of development.... 1) The first stage was a *period of patronage* by the missionary, a period of looking up to him as the big boss, the last word on every subject.... 2) The second stage coincided with the rising tide of nationalism in the country and was one of *bitter*

hostility to the missionary. He was accused of having a superiority complex, of keeping down the Indian, and of having an unsympathetic attitude toward Indian culture. 3) Fortunately, this period of hostility had a constructive side to it. The relationship enters a new stage in the post-independence period where the dominant desire is to meet on a *footing of equality* and work together for the common good. (Blaise Levai, *Revolution in Missions,* The Popular Press, p. 263)

The role of a particular missionary at the present time depends, of course, on the status of the church where he or she is working. There are some missionaries working in primitive tribal areas (as in the mountains of New Guinea) who are still in the pioneering period of missions. They are majoring on evangelism and laying foundations for the future church. Others are still in the administrative stage. The church where they are serving is still in its infancy and has not had sufficient time to develop its own leadership. So missionaries are still acting as supervisors and managers. But in a great number of areas, where Christian missions have been in operation for fifty or even a hundred years, missionaries are now in the final stage of partner or fellow-worker, serving under the direction of the national church. This is the situation with most of the mainline mission boards today.

However, it must be pointed out that there is a growing feeling among many mission leaders in the United States that the time has come for all mission boards to pull up stakes in those areas where the church has been sufficiently established and to get back to pioneer missions in the areas where there is no church. At least they should concentrate the majority of their personnel in such sections of the world. This promises to be one of the most significant movements in Christian missions in the days ahead. More will be said about this in a later chapter.

Relationship between Mission and Church
While the relationship of missionary to national church has been undergoing changes, the relationship of the mission board to the national church has also changed. During the

pioneer period of missions, there was no church (no Christians, no congregations), only "the mission." Each missionary was a *sent one*, sent out by some mission board in Europe or America, without any reference to the field. Then as people were won to Christ and congregations were formed, the mission gave birth to the church. The relationship between the two was that of parent and child. The parent was responsible to nurture and train the child, supplying all its needs, paying all its bills, and making all its decisions.

But a day came when the child, the national church, grew up and became an adult. No longer was it willing to be treated as a child. It wanted to express its own selfhood and make its own decisions. So the relationship between mission and church changed to that of brother to brother or sister to sister. Both were born of the same Spirit, shared the same blood and heritage, and were on an equal footing. Missionaries and nationals became coworkers and partners under God. Today's missionary is no longer just a *sent one*, sent out by the foreign mission board. The missionary is a *called-and-sent-one*, called by the national church and sent out by the church back home. No longer can a mission society "dump" a number of missionaries on the national church; it must respond to the invitation of the national church for specific personnel to fill specific assignments.

So the situation today is something like this: the personnel committee of a particular national church decides how many missionaries to ask for and where they are needed. For example, a nurse is needed in this village clinic; a professor of Old Testament in that particular seminary; an agriculturalist for this rural center; an evangelist-church planter for that new area; and so on. Then the mission board takes that list and recruits personnel with proper training and experience to fill those posts. At the end of each term on the field, leaders of the national church reevaluate the character and service of the missionary, and recommend his or her return or nonreturn to the field.

National Christians are insisting more and more on their right to specify what type of missionaries are recruited and to participate in the screening process. At times boards have been known to send out missionaries who were unacceptable to the church on the field. Those who are recruited should be willing to assume the servant role, to cooperate with leaders on the field, to identify themselves with its people and culture, and to learn as well as instruct. Missionaries of today must be willing to place themselves at the disposal of the national church. Their attitude should be, "Here I am; what do you want me to do?" They must be willing to accept an appointment given to them by national leaders, and be ready to serve "under" them in a spirit of equality and partnership.

Thus missionaries now have a two-way relationship—to the sending church and the receiving church. They hear the command to "go" and respond to the invitation to "come over and help us."

Partnership in obedience is a fitting slogan to express the new relationship between Western and Eastern churches. It involves several important ideas. Partnership in obedience regards the churches of Africa and Asia as real churches in themselves, and not merely as "outstations" or dependencies of Western churches. It regards the relationship between missionaries and nationals as that of partnership and cooperation.

Partnership in obedience recognizes that both East and West are responsible for congregations being built up and that both are responsible for taking the Gospel to all peoples. The Great Commission is binding on every church around the world.

Partnership also means that the churches of East and West have decided not to exist independently of each other, but to pool their resources in finances and personnel in order to fulfill the Great Commission in our generation. To achieve this, it is of course necessary that each one of the partners seek the cooperation of the other. It means that those churches that have been only *receiving* churches must now become *sending* churches as well; and those that have been only *sending* churches should learn to *receive.*

Arguments against Missionaries
Because the role of the missionary has changed in recent decades, some Christian leaders in the United States argue

that the need for the missionary has also changed. They actually proclaim that the day of foreign missions is past. This conviction is reflected in the serious decrease in the number of missionaries being sent out by the mainline denominational mission boards. Twenty years ago the United Methodist Church had about 1,500 persons serving abroad; today, less than 500. The number of United Presbyterian missionaries has dropped from 1,300 in 1958 to 359 in 1980. In the Lutheran Church the number has fallen to 148; in the American Baptist Churches, to 200 (1980 figures). Even in the U.S. Roman Catholic Church, the number of foreign missionaries has decreased from 9,655 in 1969 to 6,393 in 1980. Several arguments are given for reducing the number of foreign missionaries. Let us look at them briefly.

Missionaries are no longer needed today. During the past one or two hundred years, Christianity has become a universal faith. There are churches in practically every country in the world. Christians are everywhere. The job of missions has been carried out so widely and so well that we can now retire from the field with a sense of satisfaction. We can pack up our bags and come home, congratulating ourselves on having accomplished our mission. After all, is it not the aim of missionaries to put themselves out of a job?

Missionaries are no longer wanted. Many voices tell us that churches overseas no longer welcome missionaries. National leaders are grateful for what missionaries have done in the past, but are critical of their insensitive approaches and domineering attitudes. They feel that the continued presence of missionaries is now a hindrance to spiritual growth and maturity of the national church. As long as missionaries are around, they argue, the church on the field will not feel free to express itself and develop its own initiative. It would be best for missionaries to pull out and let the nationals stand on their own feet. This attitude is often attributed to the strong spirit of nationalism that is prevalent in Afro-Asian countries.

Missionaries have become too expensive. Many argue that it costs too much to support missionaries these days because of inflation both at home and abroad. It is estimated that it now costs, on the average, about $22,000 annually to keep a missionary family on the field. This includes basic salary, children's and medical allowances, plus travel to and from the field. That same amount of money, we are reminded, would support twenty or more national evangelists. Furthermore, the nationals are already on the spot, they don't have to worry about visas, they know the language, and they are part of the culture. They can to a better job than missionaries. Some mission boards claim that their incomes have not kept pace with inflation, so they are forced to reduce the number of missionaries in order to balance the budget.

Arguments for Missionaries

Now, there is just enough truth in all of these arguments to make them appear plausible on the surface. But on further investigation it is quite evident that they are based on misinformation and misunderstanding of the true mission of the church. At best they are only half-truths.

Are missionaries needed? It is true that in some sections of the worldwide church, missionaries are *not* needed. The church has been established for a long time, is blessed with capable leadership, and is well able to carry on by itself. A good example of this would be the Mar Thoma Syrian Church of Kerala, South India. This church can trace its heritage clear back to the Apostle Thomas. The Syrian Church in India is one of the older churches in Christendom and has not had permanent missionaries in its midst for decades. Likewise, some other churches across the world could be cited.

However, the fact that missionaries are not needed in some areas does not mean that they are not needed anywhere. Even some well-established churches across the seas are still needing and requesting missionaries to serve in certain specialized positions, for which they themselves do not have trained personnel. But beyond this, in vast areas in the world the Gospel has not yet been proclaimed. It is estimated that over 3 billion people are still unevangelized. The task is so big it will take the combined resources of Christian churches all over the world. Missionaries from both East and West will be necessary until Jesus comes. National leaders do not seek to escape responsibility for the evangelization of their lands, but they know they will need all the help they can get—from God and their brothers and sisters—if they are ever to confront their generation with the Good News of Jesus Christ.

In view of all this, for Christians anywhere to say, "Missionaries are not needed" is to close their eyes to the awesome task before us. No one claims that the evangelization of the world will ever be accomplished by merely increasing the number of foreign missionaries, or even by multiplying the number of national pastors in every land, though such an increase is needed. It is becoming clearer and clearer that total evangelization lies in total mobilization. All Christians everywhere must be involved in the task in some way or other—by praying, giving, witnessing, or going.

Are missionaries wanted? It is also true that in some areas of the world missionaries are not wanted today. They are certainly not wanted by some governments, which are hostile to the Christian movement and are closing or have already closed the door to foreign missionaries. They are not wanted in some church circles as well. Many national church leaders are capable of running their own show and sincerely believe they can do it better unhampered by the presence of foreigners. However, to generalize and say, "Missionaries are not wanted anywhere," is grossly misleading.

In many parts of the world, missionaries are not only wanted but *desperately* wanted. This is not merely the opinion of mission executives, but of the leaders of the national churches and of our brothers and sisters in Christ in these lands. One has only to look at the long lists of requests for missionary personnel that are sent from the fields to the home mission boards to be convinced of this fact.

In one mainline denomination, bishops from the field have been making repeated and urgent requests for missionaries for a number of years. But, sad to say, the requests have gone unheeded. In desperation, the evangelical segment of the denomination has established a new mission society, primarily to respond to these urgent demands for new missionaries.

It is true that a few years ago in some areas, particularly in Africa, a strong suggestion was made that missionaries be withdrawn, at least for a period. The reason given was that such action would encourage churches to take full responsibility and stand on their own feet. Leaders of the movement were, mostly, persons affiliated with the World Council of Churches. The Bangkok Conference of the WCC (January 1973) agreed that such a temporary suspension of funds and personnel would be advantageous to Afro-Asian churches. Later this resolution was reaffirmed by the WCC-affiliated All Africa Council of Churches, which met at Lusaka, Zambia, in May 1974.

However, this movement proved to be highly impractical. It soon became evident that wholesale withdrawal of missionaries would be disastrous in most areas and would leave many stations unmanned. Furthermore, it was realized that the objective behind the move could be achieved without the physical withdrawal of missionaries. Wherever feasible, missionaries should hand over the reins of administration to nationals and enter into a new relationship of equality and cooperation. They should encourage national leaders to assume full responsibility for their own churches and make their own decisions.

The International Congress on World Evangelization, which met in Lausanne, Switzerland in July 1974, made a very clear statement on the subject of missionary withdrawal. The Lausanne Covenant agrees that "a reduction of foreign missionaries and money . . . may sometimes be necessary." But it qualifies this statement in three important ways. First, such a situation is likely to arise only in an "evangelized country," that is, where the Gospel has been proclaimed and an indigenous church established. Second, the purpose of such a reduction would be "to facilitate the National Church's growth in self-reliance." Missionaries should avoid staying on too long in leadership roles, thereby impeding development of the national church's own leaders. Third, the ultimate objective of such a reduction would not be to reduce overall missionary advance, but to further it, for it would "release resources for unevangelized areas." We dare not impose any limit on the number of missionaries while so much of the world remains unevangelized.

In April 1969 the United Church of Japan (the Kyodan) announced that it would suspend calling evangelistic missionaries for a period of two years. The purpose was to study and reevaluate the place of missionaries in the Japanese church. It is interesting that in February 1971, after the study was completed, the Kyodan wholeheartedly decided to resume inviting missionaries from overseas, though it made some clear recommendations about spiritual and practical qualifications that missionaries should have.

It is quite clear today that the call for missionaries from abroad is coming from those national church leaders who have carefully surveyed the spiritual needs of their own lands and realistically assessed the contribution that foreign missionaries can still make to the work. They are fully aware of the missionary's limitations but deeply conscious of the demands of the unfinished task among their own people. Many mission boards testify that they are bombarded with more personnel needs than they can fill. Pressure for help is coming, not from the missionaries, but from the national churches themselves.

One more word in this regard. We must distinguish between missionaries being *needed* and their being *wanted.* There are many places where missionaries are not wanted (especially by governments hostile to Christianity) but where they are certainly needed (in view of the unfinished task). Since when have missionaries gone only to places where they are wanted? If that were the case, they would never have gone from Antioch to Syria to Asia Minor and Europe in the first place. Missionaries go where God sends them and where they are needed.

Are missionaries too expensive? As to the third argument regarding the problem of mission finances, it *is* true that inflation and the rise in the cost of living have made the support of missionaries a greater financial burden. To argue that we could support twenty or more national preachers for the price of one missionary family certainly makes a strong case. But other factors should be considered.

In the Afro-Asian churches is found a strong drive for self-support these days. It is not a healthy situation when a national pastor relies on foreign funds for his support. An accepted principle nowadays is that each congregation should support its own pastor. This is necessary for the spiritual maturity of the Christians and the financial stability of the church. Thus, the national churches will no longer accept help on pastors' salaries. They feel that this is their responsibility. Even newly formed mission societies in the national churches follow this principle. They insist that their missionaries be supported by Christians of the land. One of the frequent questions put by non-Christians in Asia these days is, Why do you use foreign money to pay national preachers to convert our people? Mission funds are still needed on the field for all kinds of projects, but not for the support of national pastors and evangelists.

Then again, if the cost of the missionary has gone up, so has the cost of everything else. But business companies don't reduce their personnel abroad and the United States government doesn't reduce its troops abroad just because it requires more money than before. They merely increase the budget. Why, then, should the missionary enterprise, one of the most significant movements in the world, reduce its forces because of finances? If missionaries are needed across the world, and needed desperately, we should raise the necessary funds to support them. After all, the amount spent on foreign missions by all the United States churches put together can't compare to the vast sums of money being spent by American people on other things. The price of one Air Force bomber would support several hundred missionaries. We spend billions of dollars on liquor and cigarettes and pennies on missions. American people spend more in one year on cosmetics, or chewing gum, or dog and cat food than they do for the spread of the Gospel of Jesus Christ around the world! Do we really believe in missions? Are we ready to sacrifice for the mission of the church?

Actually, when we look at facts, we see that the number of missionaries being sent out from the United States has increased in the past decade or two. While some mission boards have been reducing their personnel drastically, others have made great advances. For example, consider a comparison between the United Methodist Church and the Southern Baptist Convention. About twenty years ago, each of these denominations had approximately 1,500 missionaries overseas. But whereas the number of United Methodist missionaries has fallen to 516, the number of Southern Baptist missionaries has increased to 3,346. In fact, Southern Baptists have set a goal of 5,000 missionaries in the near future. Then again, compare the United Methodist Church with the Christian and Missionary Alliance. Whereas the former, with a total membership of 9 million, is supporting 516 foreign missionaries (a ratio of 1/17,440), the latter, with a membership of only 150,000, is supporting 874 missionaries (a ratio of 1/170). If the United Methodist Church had the same ratio of missionaries to members, it would support 53,000 missionaries, not just 516.

Independent "faith mission boards" and parachurch organizations seem to have much greater zeal for missions these days. Here is a 1985 list of ten of the leading sending agencies in the United States (*Missions Handbook*, 13th edition, MARC):

Southern Baptist Convention	3,346
Wycliffe Bible Translators	3,022
Youth With A Mission	1,741
New Tribes Mission	1,438
Assemblies of God	1,237
Seventh-Day Adventists	1,052
Churches of Christ	982
The Evangelical Alliance Mission	874
Christian Chs./Churches of Christ	709

Although the role of the missionary has certainly changed in many areas, missionaries are still needed and wanted around the world.

PART FOUR

CULTURAL ISSUES—What Do We Do about Culture?

The Christian movement in the past has been criticized for trying to westernize as well as evangelize the people of Africa and Asia. It has taken a plant bred in North America or Europe and sought to transplant it to other soils. Conviction has grown in recent years that our mission is to sow the seed of the Gospel and then allow it to grow according to the culture and soil of the land. We should be careful not to unnecessarily destroy a culture wholesale but seek to conserve those cultural values that are in harmony with God's will. Changes will take place, of course, but these should be brought about by the dynamic of the Gospel and not the manipulation of the missionary. The Christian message must be adapted to the cultural background of the listener in order to be more intelligible and effective. Missionaries need training in cross-cultural communication.

TEN

THE CHURCH AND CULTURE

Much discussion on the subject of the Gospel and culture has taken place in missionary circles in recent years. It is recognized that we do not preach the Gospel or plant churches in a vacuum. People do not live in isolation as individuals. They live in society, in relationship to one another, as they were created to live. Society is held together by culture, which is passed on from one generation to another and acts as a blueprint for the behavior and thinking of a people. Culture influences a people in a hundred and one different ways. It fashions their concepts of the Creator and the world around them; it establishes their values of the good and the beautiful; it determines rites and ceremonies; it establishes roles and patterns of behavior; it determines relationships and responsibilities; it is the medium God uses to communicate with His children. Culture becomes the soil in which the church is planted and determines largely what type of church it will be. Such questions naturally arise: How does culture affect the church? How does the church affect culture? What is the relationship between the two?

The Old Approach
As we look back on the missionary expansion of the past (particularly of the nineteenth century), we must admit that serious mistakes were made in regard to culture. In general, early pioneer missionaries had a positive view of their own

culture and a rather negative view of other cultures. Theirs was an *attitude of condemnation* that looked upon everything that was not Western as pagan or heathen and therefore unworthy of attention.

Several reasons can be cited for this attitude. First of all, those pioneer missionaries came up against foreign cultures in their original form, untouched by Western values. They were faced with such practices as *satti* (widow burning), infanticide, human sacrifices, temple prostitution, headhunting, and cannibalism. It was easy for the missionaries to label all this as "pagan." In addition, the science of cultural anthropology was in an infant stage and practically unknown at the time. Missionaries did not understand the significance of culture in the life of a people and the danger of making unnecessary changes or introducing changes too fast. The study of comparative religions was also new. Missionaries saw the grosser aspects of the world religions as practiced by the masses without realizing some of the ethical content of these faiths. Finally, the missionaries failed to distinguish between the Gospel and Western culture. Because of technological superiority of Western nations, and their military and political power, an attitude of cultural superiority developed: "We're civilized; others are uncivilized."

This attitude of condemnation often led to *the practice of withdrawal*—the attempt to isolate the church from its cultural environment. Missionaries felt that because the culture of the people was so pagan, it was almost impossible for Christian converts to remain in their old surroundings and live a genuine Christian life. Temptations and pressures to revert to their old customs were considered to be too strong for new believers to withstand. So early missionaries extracted the converts from their former society and gathered them in Christian ghettos or mission stations in order to provide support systems for their new way of life.

The practice of withdrawal in turn led to *the practice of imposition*—the attempt to impose Western culture upon converts. Since foreign culture was considered pagan and Western culture was considered Christian, missionaries naturally sought to spread European culture. Some missionaries, for a time, actually believed that Western civilization was a preparation for Christianity. Thus it was generally assumed that churches on the mission field would be modeled on churches at home. Their tendency was to produce almost exact replicas. Gothic architecture, prayer-book liturgies, clerical dress, musical instruments, hymns and tunes, standards for ordination, and organizational forms (from committees to bishops to general conferences)—all were exported and dumped on the new mission-founded churches. It is true that these patterns were also eagerly adopted by the new Christians, who wanted to keep up with their European friends. But all this was based on the false assumptions that the Bible gave specific instructions about these matters and that these Western patterns were in themselves exemplary.

Several ill effects of this approach are evident. Such a negative attitude toward culture unnecessarily tore down much that was of real value in foreign cultures. Virtues are found in every culture, and these need to be preserved. To undermine them is to bring harm to the whole social fabric, to destroy the very foundation that gives meaning and purpose to people's lives.

This old approach also hindered effective communication of the Gospel. We added Western incidentals to Gospel essentials, which made it difficult for people to understand and accept the message. I once met a Brahmin Hindu in India who told me he was seriously interested in becoming a Christian but was reluctant to do so because he would have to eat beef. When I asked him what eating beef had to do with becoming a Christian, he said that a missionary had told him that if he became a Christian, he should be willing to eat beef to demonstrate that he was "finished with the old ways and ideas." He was greatly relieved when I told him he could be a vegetarian Christian, if he so desired, and that eating beef was not an integral part of the Christian life. How often we have turned people away from the Gospel by wrapping it in a Western cultural package!

In addition, the old negative attitude toward culture prevented establishing a truly indigenous church. We failed to permit national churches to express their Christianity in the genius of their own culture. By imposing our Western patterns on them, we made Christianity look like a foreign religion to people outside the church. They felt that in order to become Christians they had to adopt a strange culture in which they did not feel at home. Furthermore, creativity of the Christian church was stifled, since they were not free to develop their own style of music or worship or government. Confusing Christianity with Western culture is unbiblical and prevents people from seeing how Christ can become a living, vibrant force in their own culture.

The New Approach
Our new attitude is to look upon the social and cultural environment of the people not as an obstacle to be overcome but as a storehouse of the finest treasures that people have amassed in their struggle toward self-fulfullment. It is the task of the church to conserve the values of a society as much as possible and weave them into the structure of the church. This is not an easy task; it is a delicate and costly process. But it must be done if the church is to endure as a Japanese or Indian or African and not as an American or European institution.

The objective of the Christian mission is *to Christianize not to westernize.* We sometimes forget the wide difference between the two and think that to introduce Christianity means also to introduce Western ways. The great missionary Paul set us a notable example in this regard. He went forth to evangelize, not to Judaize. He was careful to distinguish between the essential Gospel and the culture of a particular group.

The Task of the Church
The church of Jesus Christ has a threefold duty with regard to its social environment.

The church must seek to understand the culture of a people and its significance in their lives. This means that we will discover not only *what* people do, but *why* they do it—reasons behind their behavior. The reason may not always justify the action, but at least it helps us to understand how people think and to find the proper solution for the problem.

Consider, for example, the practice of polygamy, which is

found in many tribal societies in Africa. As Westerners we tend to judge polygamy from the standpoint of sex: the more wives a man has, the more sexual pleasure he has. But that is not the reason for polygamy in the mind of the African. For a tribal chief, having several wives is a status symbol; it is expected of him. For a husband who has no children, taking a second wife in order to produce a family (or a son) is quite legitimate. An overworked wife feels free to ask her husband to take another wife in order to divide up her labor. When an African man dies, his culture expects that his younger brother will take the widow and children into his home to shelter and protect them. None of these reasons has anything to do with sex. They are all social or economic in nature. So if the church wants to deal with polygamy, it will have to find socioeconomic solutions for the problem.

I was visiting in a village in India one day when I heard a mother call out to her five-year-old daughter, "Tippavva, come here." *Tippavva* in the Kanarese language of India literally means "Miss Garbage Pile." Immediately I thought, *What a terrible name for such a beautiful little girl!* So I suggested that the mother change the *i* to a *u* and call the girl "Tuppavva," meaning "Miss Honey" (from the honeycomb). I thought I was being smart. But the mother became very upset and chided me. Later I asked my Indian fellow preacher the reason for this strange reaction to my seemingly harmless suggestion. The preacher explained that the reason the mother had given such an ugly name to the daughter was to keep evil spirits from taking notice of the beautiful child and trying to harm her. An attractive name like the one I had suggested would only make the daughter prey to evil spirits, in the mother's mind. No wonder she was upset!

We have to be very careful not to make judgments on certain behaviors or patterns until we can see and understand things from the perspective of people who practice them.

The church should conserve the values of the culture. Today it is generally accepted that the indigenous ways of life should be disturbed as little as possible. Of course, customs must be changed when they run counter to the nature and concepts of the Gospel or when they result in injustice or unnecessary hardship. But those forces in the culture that are not opposed to God's will should be used as instruments for building His church.

The Christian faith must be allowed to express itself in the cultural patterns of the country. It is not our business to take a form of Christianity grown in America and transplant it somewhere else. Rather, our task is to sow the seed of the Gospel in a given area and let it grow in accordance with the soil and climate of the land. There will always be only one Christian faith, but there will be many Christianities. Some of the areas in which it is natural for people to express their cultural references are art, architecture, worship, music, methods of evangelism, and forms of government.

During my missionary career in India I encouraged many new converts to write their own hymns and set them to Indian music. Some of the lyrics were very simple, but they came out of the hearts of the people; and they sang them with great enthusiasm. Christians wrote Gospel songs centering on the life and teachings of Jesus. Parables such as the Sower, the Good Samaritan, and the Prodigal Son were all put into poetic form and set to music. So also scenes from the life of Jesus—His birth, temptations, miracles, death, and resurrection. I also watched Christians develop their own art forms as they built their village churches. A lotus flower symbolizes purity; an oil lamp, the Christian's influence; an elephant, the inner strength of the believer. The cross, symbolizing Christ's vicarious death, is always present.

In every culture we can find values that need to be preserved. These are gifts of God's grace to a culture. In Asian countries, for example, there is a beautiful spirit of hospitality. They will always serve visitors tea and biscuits or some fruit. No matter how poor a family is, they will always have something to set before their guests. Then there is the marvelous patience of Indian people, which never ceases to amaze me. Often in India, for some reason or other, I have been delayed in arriving for a village function as much as three or four hours. But the people were always there, waiting patiently with smiles and no words of grumbling. People in the East also portray a great respect for their elders. Children are taught to obey their parents, and old people are looked up to for their experience and wisdom. In addition, the art of meditation is more highly developed in Asian countries than in the West. We are too busy for a regular devotional life, but they are quite willing to sit in silence and meditate on God and spiritual things. All of these virtues can be carried over into the life of the church and developed for the glory of God.

Certain institutions and practices of the people can be modified and Christianized so as to conserve their values and weave them into the texture of the church. This is a difficult and delicate task, demanding insight, common sense, thought and prayer, and the guidance of the Holy Spirit.

Among Buddhist people where ancestor worship is very important, the church has sought to hold memorial services for loved ones who have passed on. In this way they have done away with the actual worship of, but have retained the respect for, ancestors. In Africa, the church has turned the pagan death watch into the Christian all-night watch. When there is a death in a home, instead of beating drums all night and sitting around wailing and moaning, Christians spend the night reading Scriptures, singing hymns, praying, and sharing memories of the deceased. The fear of death displayed at a pagan funeral gives way to Christ's victory over death and the Christian's hope of the future life.

In India, two Methodist missionaries, Rev. M.D. Ross and Rev. E.A. Seamands (my father), demonstrated in a beautiful way how the Hindu *jathra* (festival), a religious institution deeply ingrained in the culture of the land, could be modified and turned into the Christian jathra. All across India, one can witness great annual Hindu festivals, where countless pilgrims come from miles around to a special place to worship at some famous idol or shrine. Most of the jathras, or festivals, are held along the banks of a river or stream. Entire families make the journey together, by bullock cart, on foot, or by train, and camp out for a few days under trees. Each family does its own cooking on an outdoor fireplace. The pilgrims worship at the shrine, carry out their various religious ceremonies, and visit friends and relatives.

So Ross and Seamands decided to hold a Christian jathra.

They chose several acres of woodland on the banks of a small stream near the town of Dharur and invited the Christians to come apart for a period of spiritual worship and renewal. As in the Hindu jathra, the Christians came by families with their own rations, cooked their meals, and slept out under the trees. Of course, there was no idol or shrine on the spot, but the living God was present in grace and power. Three services were held each day, with emphasis on evangelistic preaching and indigenous music. Dharur Jathra has now grown in attendance from 120 the first year to 100,000 in 1985 and has become the spearhead of the evangelistic movement in South India and Hyderabad Conferences of the Methodist Church in India. Thousands have found Christ as personal Saviour and have been filled with the Spirit as a result of the Dharur religious festival.

It is the duty of the church to transform the social and cultural environment by making it conformable to the will of God and a suitable place in which the Christian life may be lived. Jesus came to save individuals by spiritual rebirth and also to redeem society from evil. In one sense the church of Christ always stands against the culture in which it is placed. Cultures are products of humanity and as such partake of human frailty and sinfulness. Some elements in every culture need to be purged. Idolatry, prostitution, infanticide, head-hunting, homosexuality, pornography, and others are all contrary to the will of God and harmful to human society. A whole new set of Christian values and practices will have to replace the old forms. This is true across the seas as well as at home in the United States.

The Christian Gospel is one of the most revolutionary forces in society around the world. Wherever the love of God and the lordship of Christ have been proclaimed, they have produced significant change in both individual and corporate life. The Gospel has introduced a new sense of human dignity and the value of the individual, lifted the status of women, developed compassion for the poor and oppressed, and stimulated unselfish service for others.

We must remember two important things regarding social change. First, it is the Gospel itself, working in the hearts and minds of people and not manipulation by the missionary that brings about change. It is not the missionary's business to sit on the sideline and arbitrarily say to new converts, "This must go; that must go. You must change here; you must change there." Sometimes missionaries try to change things that don't really need to be changed, and sometimes they completely miss areas that really need to be changed. It is their task to bring people into a saving relationship with Jesus Christ and ground them in the Word of God and Christian principles. Then the Holy Spirit will guide the new converts as to what the will of God is for their personal lives and social relationships.

We also have to realize that there must be a cultural substitute for everything that is purged from a culture. Each ceremony or institution in a culture usually develops in response to some important emotional or psychological need of the people. Thus, when a particular behavior or pattern is eliminated and nothing put in its place, a vacuum develops in the lives of the people, and that is dangerous. Very often converts will revert to their old ways simply out of desperation to fill the void. For example, many non-Western people are used to handling such crises as sickness and tragedy by going to the shaman or diviner for counsel. When they are converted to Christ, they are led to understand that Christians put their trust *not* in local healers but in Christ in times of distress. But if they haven't been instructed how to handle such crises in a Christian way, then when they arise, they will rely on traditional methods. So back to the witch doctor they go, instead of drawing on such Christian resources as prayer, the Word of God, pastoral counsel, or medical skill.

Before my father and M.D. Ross inaugurated the annual Christian jathra, new converts were continuing to attend Hindu jathras, not in order to worship idols, but simply because they enjoyed the fellowship with friends and relatives that the festivals provided. But once the Christian jathra was established, both needs for Christian worship and fellowship were satisfied, and believers ceased going to the old jathras.

This principle works right here at home. If we tell our young people in the churches, "Don't drink, don't take drugs, don't smoke, don't play pool or cards," then we must provide viable alternatives for wholesome recreation. We must respond to the need for fun and recreation. Something has to fill the emotional and psychological void.

Our Need for Discernment

In summing up this discussion, we need to point out the need for caution in this matter of church and culture. On the one hand, we must avoid wholesale condemnation of the culture of a people, just because their customs and practices are strange to us. That a culture is different doesn't mean that it is inferior. There are good and bad elements in every culture. On the other hand, we must avoid indiscriminately accommodating the Christian faith to the culture of a people without any attempt to distinguish between the purely cultural and the moral. This will only lead to syncretism, the mixing of Christianity with pagan elements, which is a reproach to the Gospel. I stood one day near a church in the bazaar of Chichicastenango, Guatemala and watched an Indian go through his worship. He made a sacrifice and burned incense at a stone altar on the steps of the church while he recited incantations to the Mayan gods. Then he entered the church and recited a prayer to Mary, while he lighted candles as an offering to the "saints." This is just one example of a form of Christo-paganism found in many parts of Latin America.

The church must be both Christian and indigenous. It can be one without the other. It may be truly Christian in doctrine, and yet be a replica of Western Christianity in its forms and worship patterns. Or, it may be fully indigenous, using all the local forms and practices, but at the same time surrensurrendering the true nature of the Gospel. The church must be *rooted in Christ* and *related to the culture.*

ELEVEN

COMMUNICATION AND CULTURE

Another area in which an understanding of culture plays a significant role in Christian missions is that of communication. The missionary is a person with a message, a very important message that must be transmitted effectively. Most Christians on the home front are unaware of how difficult a task this is for the missionary. Communication is relatively easy when you address people who speak the same language and come from the same background. But when your listeners speak a foreign language and come from an entirely different social and cultural background, it's another matter altogether.

On the surface, communication appears to be a fairly easy process. It involves only three essential factors: the speaker, the message, and the listener. That's simple enough. The problem, however, is that what the speaker says and what the listener hears are not always the same thing, and so the message is misunderstood. The reason is that people have mental filters through which they sift all messages that come their way. These filters are made up of language forms, religious views, and cultural values as well as people's life experiences. So the missionary doesn't pour the Christian message into an empty vessel, but rather into a vessel that already contains certain assumptions, beliefs, prejudices, and attitudes. All these influence the way the listener understands the message.

For an example right here at home, suppose a preacher tries to compare God to an earthly father, and there is a young man in the congregation who has an alcoholic father, who wastes the family income on liquor and often beats his wife and children. When the young man hears the word *father,* he puts it through the filter of his experiences, and immediately says to himself, "If God is like my father, I don't want anything to do with Him!"

Now look at an example across the seas. Among the Zanaki people of Tanzania, Africa, only thieves knock on doors. They approach a house in the middle of the night, knock on the doorposts, and then hide in the bushes to see if there is any movement within. If the people are at home, they dash off into the darkness. If there is no response, they stay and plunder the house. An honest man will stand outside the house and call out the names of the people inside. Thus, when the Zenaki people hear the missionary quoting Revelation 3:20, "Behold I stand at the door and knock," they conclude that Jesus is a thief.

We dare not assume that hearing the Gospel is the same thing as understanding the Gospel. True communication takes place only when a message has been given and the intended point has been grasped by the listener. This means that missionaries must understand the listener's point of view and way of thinking. In order to do this, they must step away from their own cultural background, cross over onto the cultural ground of the people, and stand on their level.

Here is where God Himself is our model. He is the Master Communicator. When He wanted to communicate His nature, His will, His love to us, He didn't demand that we become angels and learn His heavenly language. He chose the path of the incarnation and stepped over onto our turf. He did all the adjusting, allowing us to remain on familiar ground. Through the person of Christ, God became a human person, spoke a human language, and identified Himself with a particular society. It was out of love and respect for us that He was willing to come down to our level. Christian messengers today must follow this principle if they are to be effective communicators of God's message to the world. It is not an easy task, but it is necessary.

In cross-cultural communication the Christian missionary faces problems in three areas.

Problems Arising from Language

Differences in language construction. Each language has its own word order and style of expression, so that what goes well in one language may not work in another. An American evangelist preaching in Africa through an interpreter explained at the outset of his sermon that he was going to preach on the "four ships." The interpreter translated it literally, using the local word for *ship* or *boat.* Then the speaker went on to discuss the "four ships"—relationship, fellowship, partnership, and stewardship. Of course, when the interpreter translated these words into the African language, none of them ended with *ship.* The sermon outline fell flat.

Several times I have used an outline for a sermon on temptation that I heard Dr. Paul Rees use on one occasion. It goes like this: Temptation will *come.* Temptation may be *overcome.* Temptation *overcome* leads to a glorious *outcome.* It is a catchy play on the word *come.* But it is based on the English language, and when translated into some other language, it immediately loses its force. Some sermon outlines and forms that we use in English cannot be used effectively in Hindi, Swahili, Korean, or Japanese. We have to develop a whole new set of outlines that are based on the language in which we are communicating.

Differences in word meanings. A word may have different meanings to different groups of people. To Americans the word *bonnet* means a head covering used by women and children; to the English it can mean the hood of an automobile. When Americans say, "I want to wash up," they're talking about washing their hands before a meal; when the English use the phrase, they're referring to washing dishes after a meal.

Meanings are attached to words by people. They remain the same when people continue to use words in the same way; they change when people decide to use words in different ways. The word *prevent* once meant to precede or go before; in present-day English it means to obstruct or stop from doing. The word *gay* used to mean merry or cheerful; now it also refers to a homosexual lifestyle.

Christian messengers cannot take for granted that their listeners are giving the same meaning to words as they are. For example, to the Christian, *sin* means a willful transgression of God's moral law; to the Hindu, it means ignorance or illusion. To the Christian, *salvation* means deliverance from the guilt and power of sin; to the Hindu, it means deliverance from the cycle of birth and rebirth. The phrase *new birth* to the Christian means spiritual transformation; to the Hindu, it means reincarnation, being born as an animal or human person in the next life. This is why it is so important for the missionary to know the language of the people and the meanings they attach to words that are commonly used.

Limitation in vocabulary. Sometimes the local language does not possess words for some of the basic concepts of the Gospel, such as repentance, faith, love, sin, salvation, and sanctification. In the language of the Motilones, a remote tribe in Colombia, South America, there is no word for sin. One has to name specific wrong deeds, such as lying, stealing, killing, etc. The only way to express the idea of love is to say, "My stomach is hungry for you; I want to eat you." "Conversion" is described as "leaving the devil's trail and starting on God's trail." *To have faith* or *believe* is translated "to walk on God," which really describes the faith that a Motilone must exercise when he walks across a stream on a slippery log bridge. When a Motilone becomes a Christian, he or she "gets a new language" or "has Jesus talk in his mouth." This means the person has received a new life.

In the language of the Dogons, a tribe in Mali, West Africa, there is no word for conscience. Missionaries had to coin a word—*heart-knowledge.* There is no word for love, so John 3:16 has to be translated, "You are important to God, so God gave His Son."

Repentance, which connotes a profound transformation involving a change of mind, will, and heart, is translated into Kekchi of Guatemala, "it pains my heart." In Baouli, West Africa, the same idea is expressed as "it hurts so much I want to quit." In the northern Sotho language of South Africa, it is described as "it becomes untwisted." The Chols of southern

Mexico speak of "my heart is turning itself back." In all of these adaptations, we can readily see that the main idea of repentance is retained, which, after all, is the important issue.

In his book *Message and Mission* (Harper and Brothers), Dr. Eugene Nida tells us that in Nilotic Shilluk of Africa, the only way to express forgiveness is literally, "God spat on the ground in front of us." This idiom arises from the practice of plaintiffs and defendants having to spit on the ground in front of each other when finally a case has been tried, punishments meted out, and fines paid. The spitting symbolizes that the case is closed, that all is forgiven, and that the accusations cannot come into court again (p. 194).

Differences in language can certainly provide many problems for the Christian messenger, but through mastery of the language and wise adaptation of words and phrases, these barriers can be overcome. Each language possesses its own distinct genius, which can become the vehicle of transmitting God's Word. The missionary must make use of all the idioms, thought patterns, and descriptive powers of the language in order to effectively communicate the truth of God's revelation.

Problems Arising from Culture

Cultural differences. Variations in the customs, lifestyle, value system portions, and attitudes of a people are ever-present barriers to communication.

The Twenty-third Psalm is one of our favorite portions of Scripture. But to mountain people of New Guinea, the psalm is meaningless, for they have never seen a sheep and have no shepherds in their society. In fact, they don't even have a word for sheep. The same would be true of the Eskimos of Alaska, who live in a land of snow and ice and are not surrounded by "green pastures." Likewise, the Parable of the Prodigal Son which Jesus narrated is one of our favorite stories and certainly wonderful subject matter for a sermon. But to some isolated mountain people around the world, the parable poses problems. In their cultures a son does not ask for his inheritance. Furthermore, even if he received his inheritance, there would be no place to where the young man could run and spend his money in riotous living.

I remember the first time I narrated this parable to a group of orthodox Hindus in an Indian village. I pictured graphically the young man as he went off into the far country and lived a life of sensual delight. After he had spent everything he had, he ended up among the pigs, eating their husks. Finally he came to himself and decided to go back home. I could see interest in the faces of the listeners. Then I went on to describe the joyful reunion between father and son, and ended by saying, "The Father was so beside himself with joy that he called his servants and said to them, "My son has returned. It is time to celebrate. We must have a great feast tonight. Go out and kill the fatted calf!" And suddenly I noticed the look of shock that swept across the faces of my listeners. For Hindus consider the cow as sacred, and eating beef is repulsive to them. I realized I had blown the whole story. The next time I told the parable before a Hindu audience, I substituted a feast of delectable Indian dishes, thus bringing the story to a beautiful climax rather than a tragic letdown.

Another illustration of cultural barriers may be found in the story of the Sawi tribe of Irian Jaya, western New Guinea, as narrated by missionary Don Richardson in his fascinating book *Peace Child* (Regal Books). When Richardson studied the culture of this stone-age tribe, he soon discovered that this people idealized treachery as a virtue, a goal of life. They not only were cruel but honored cruelty. They found their highest pleasure in the misery and despair of others. They were not satisfied with overt killing—suddenly pouncing upon and slaying a lone warrior from another tribe who had carelessly wandered into their territory. They practiced a more sophisticated style of treachery, carefully and artfully carried out over a period of time. They would gradually win the trust of their intended victim by showering him with praise and gifts, and inviting him to several feasts in their homes. Finally one day, while the unsuspecting warrior was eating and laughing merrily, the Sawi men would pounce on him with their stone axes and spears and with shouts of glee slaughter him. They would cut his body into pieces with sharp bamboo knives, cook it, and eat it. This whole process was called "fattening with friendship for the kill."

Thus, it happened that as the missionary was narrating the details of the life of Christ to the Sawi people, when he came to the description of Judas Iscariot's betrayal of the Son of God, he noticed that they listened with unusual interest and admiration. They chuckled with glee, whistled birdcalls, and touched their chests in awe. Suddenly Richardson realized they were acclaiming Judas as the hero of the story! In their thinking, Judas had done nothing wrong; in fact, he was a super Sawi! They had never heard such a fantastic tale of "fattening with friendship for the kill." And Christ, the object of Judas' treachery, meant nothing to these men.

Cultural adaptations. By adapting the Christian message to the cultural patterns of a people, missionaries can achieve effective communication. What is actually involved is not altering the essential content of the biblical message, but putting it in a form that can be understood by listeners. We have no right to change the meaning of the Gospel—that would be a betrayal of our trust—but we have an obligation to make the message plain to the hearers. This is exactly what God did through Jesus; He spelled Himself out in language people could understand. The fact is, because of cultural differences, there are times when the form of the message *must* be different if the content of the message is to be true.

Among the mountain people of New Guinea, there is no such thing as bread, so they have no word for bread. The staple food of these people is the sweet potato, which they eat two or three times a day, day in and day out. So the words of Jesus, "I am the bread of life" (John 6:48) are translated "I am the sweet potato of life." This, of course, conveys the real meaning of the words of Jesus and makes sense to those people of New Guinea. Likewise, in the statement of Jesus, "No one who puts his hand to the plow and looks back is fit for the kingdom of God" (Luke 9:62), the word *plow* has to be changed to *hoe*, for these mountain people have never seen a plow. They make use of a crude hoe in their gardening. Then again, in the words of John the Baptist, "Behold the Lamb of God, who takes away the sin of the world" (John 1:29), the phrase *pig of God* has to be substituted, for there are no sheep or lambs in the area. The pig, however, is to the people of New Guinea as the lamb was to the people of ancient Israel.

We Westerners talk about the emotional focus of the personality as the "heart." A young man says to his girlfriend, "I love you with all my *heart.*" But this is by no means a universal practice. In some parts of the world the young man would have to say, "I love you with all my *stomach*" or "with all my *liver.*" In a number of languages in Africa, John 14:1 is translated, "Let not your *livers* be troubled."

The book *Peace Child,* which was just mentioned, not only gives an illustration of cultural barriers to communication, but also offers a fine illustration of evangelizing a people by applying scriptural truth to their cultural patterns. When Don Richardson saw the reaction of the Sawi warriors to the narration of Judas Iscariot's betrayal of the Son of God, he was absolutely dumbfounded. How could he possibly get the Sawis to understand the significance of the death of Christ? How could he reverse their whole thinking in the light of their particular worldview? But one day God showed him the way.

Because of the helpfulness of Richardson and his wife, who was a nurse, two Sawi clans had built villages close to each other in order to benefit from the medical and technical skills of the missionaries. But as time went on, they began to fight with each other, and several lives were lost. Finally, when their hostility came to a climax and it looked like a full-scale battle would ensue, Richardson called the leaders of the two clans together and announced that he and his wife had decided to leave in order to make way for the clans to separate from each other and stop the killing. The stunned leaders went off into a huddle; and after a tumult of discussion, they returned and said to the missionary, "Don't leave us. We're not going to kill each other anymore. Tomorrow we are going to sprinkle cool water on each other" (that is, make peace).

The following morning the missionary couple witnessed an unusual and perplexing ceremony. The leading warriors of both clans gathered in the clearing of the jungle, facing each other from a distance. Behind each group of men stood the women and children. The atmosphere was fraught with tension and excitement. Suddenly one of the men from one side grabbed his baby boy from the arms of his wife. The mother screamed and tried to hold on to the child, but the father ran to the other side. When the man reached the other group, he handed his baby over to one of the warriors and said, "I give you my son and with him my name. Plead the words of my people among your people. Let us live in peace!"

The other man gently received the child and answered, "It is enough! I will surely plead peace between us." Then all the members of the clan filed by, one by one, and laid hands on the child, sealing their acceptance of the peace bargain.

Then the identical scene was repeated from the other side. One of the warriors wrenched his six-month-old son from the arms of his terrified wife, ran across the opening and handed him over to the enemy. Then both parties carried off the newly adopted sons to their own respective villages to decorate them for the peace celebration. Meanwhile young men stuck feathers in their hair, brought out their drums, and began to dance.

All the while, the missionaries looked on in horror and amazement. They thought, *What will happen now? Will the two babies be chopped into pieces, cooked, and eaten?* Richardson called one of the warriors aside and asked, "What are they going to do? What does all this mean?"

Exuberantly, the Sawi warrior answered, "Missionary, you have been urging us to make peace. Don't you know it is impossible to have peace without a *peace child?*" Then he went on to explain that if a man would actually give his son to his enemies, that man could be trusted. It was an unquestionable proof of his goodwill, his sincere desire for reconciliation and peace. And everyone who laid his hand on the son was bound to live in peace with those who gave him, as long as the son lived. To kill the *peace child* would be the crime of all crimes. The man assured the missionary that the two babies would not be harmed; in fact, both villages would guard the lives of these children even more zealously than the lives of their own offspring.

When he heard this, Richardson's horror suddenly turned to excitement. The living peace child was a culturally built-in antidote to the Sawi idealization of violence. This was the key he had been praying for! Two months later, after he was convinced that the peace treaty was working effectively, he called the elders of the clans together and addressed them.

"You are right! You can't make peace without the painful giving of a son. But long before you discovered this truth, God knew it. So because He wants all men to find peace with Him and with each other, He decided to give His only Son, Jesus, as a *Peace Child* to the world. To reject God's Peace Child is the greatest of all sins. But when we accept Him, we can live at peace with God as long as the Son is alive—which means forever!"

For the first time the light of the Gospel broke into the darkness of the Sawi mind. The hero of the Gospel narrative was no longer Judas, but Jesus! Jesus was God's *Peace Child,* and Judas had planned his death! The Sawis concluded, "We must be careful not to commit the same sin!"

What was the result? After a few months of further instruction and prayer on the part of the missionary, these two entire clans of the Sawi people laid their hands on God's Peace Child and sealed their acceptance of His gift. Today they are all disciples of Christ, worshiping in their dome-shaped sanctuary and singing the praises of their Redeemer.

Don Richardson ends his story of the conversion of the Sawi people with this magnificent conviction: *that God, down through the centuries, has been building into the culture of every tribe and people redemptive analogies for the effective communication of the Gospel!* Herein lies the key to their hearts and to their conversion. And so God is looking for messengers who are willing to go and live among the world's untouched people, identify with their struggles and aspirations, learn their language and culture, and discover the redemptive analogy that will enable them to understand the matchless love and grace of our blessed Redeemer. This is what missionary work is all about!

Problems Arising from Religion

Of all the barriers to communication of the Gospel of Christ to people of other cultures, the religious barriers are perhaps the most difficult to overcome. Sometimes there are teachings in the non-Christian religious systems that are contrary to the teaching of the Bible and that therefore make it difficult for people to understand or accept the truth of the Gospel. To illustrate this problem we will deal with the main concepts of just two world religions—Islam and Hinduism.

Islam. Islam holds certain theological ideas that cut right across the basic truths of Christianity. In the first place, Islam emphasizes the *unity* of God, and thus has great problems with the idea of the Trinity in Christianity. Muslims accuse Christians of believing in three gods and therefore of practicing idolatry. The difficulty arises because Muslims think of the Trinity in a physical sense: God had a wife (perhaps Mary), and they had sexual intercourse and gave birth to a son, Jesus. Naturally, all of this appears as sheer blasphemy.

The first responsibility of the Christian missionary is to clear up the misunderstanding. He must state that Christians do not believe in three Gods, but only one God in three persons or functions. He must assert that God did *not* marry. He never marries and has no need to marry. When Muslims hear this, they immediately feel greatly relieved and assume a much more relaxed attitude in conversation.

The doctrine of the Trinity is indeed difficult for anyone to understand. The fact of the matter is that when we try to explain divine mysteries in human language, we get just so far and then can go no farther. Christian evangelists have used various illustrations in attempting to explain the Trinity to Muslims, but each one has its limitations. Some use the illustration of the egg, which has three parts—shell, yolk, and white—but is one single object. Others point out that a man may have three different roles—as father, son, and doctor—but he is still one person.

Perhaps the best way to explain the Trinity to a Muslim is to ask the questions, "Are you a living body? Are you a living mind? Are you a living soul?" When the person answers yes, ask, "Which of the three is you?" He or she will naturally say, "I am all three." Then it can be pointed out that each one of us is a trinity on the human level, and yet we regard ourselves as one. Somehow, in some mysterious way beyond our comprehension, the Godhead is three and yet one. If we deny the divine Trinity, we also deny the human personality.

In the second place, Islam emphasizes strongly the *sovereignty* of God and because of this denies two of the most important events of the Christian faith—the incarnation and the crucifixion. The idea of incarnation is something difficult for Muslims to accept, for they feel it is unthinkable that the sovereign ruler of the universe would stoop to become a mere man. That is simply below His dignity. Muslims contend that God will reveal His will through a book and through prophets but never in person. Jesus was not the "Son of God," but only a prophet. To speak of Him as the Son of God is to be guilty of *shirk* (making someone coequal with God), which is the most deadly of all sins.

Furthermore, on the basis of God's sovereignty, Muslims deny outright the death of Christ on the cross. The Koran clearly states: "They did not kill him, but it appeared so to them" (Sura 4:158). Most Muslims believe that God took Jesus to heaven just before the crucifixion and that a substitute, perhaps Judas, was crucified in His place. It is unthinkable to Muslims that God would allow His prophet to be scourged, spat upon, and crucified between two thieves. God always vindicates His prophets with victory. So it is impossible that such a good man as Jesus should die, for God is all-powerful and would certainly have saved Him from this horrible death. Then again, the atonement was unnecessary, for God can forgive sins by His own sovereign act.

In meeting these objections, Christian missionaries can take their stand on the very sovereignty of God that Muslims accept. If God is truly sovereign, can He not *choose* to become a man and reveal Himself in person? Who are we to deny Him that right? If God can speak through human language—Arabic—why not through human personality? Which is the greater revelation? A book or a life?

Again, it is exactly on the basis of God's sovereignty that Christians can affirm the crucifixion. If God is really sovereign, can He not *choose* to make the cross the means of our redemption? Who are we to tell Him how He should manage His affairs? Furthermore, it is because God is sovereign that the atonement became necessary. He cannot forgive sin lightly with just a wave of His hand. There would be no moral quality in such cheap forgiveness. But through the cross He upheld His moral law and dealt radically with sin. Now he offers forgiveness in a nail-pierced hand, a forgiveness with real moral content.

We can ask Muslims: Which is the greater victory for Almighty God? To snatch Jesus away at the last moment and rescue Him from death? Or to allow Him to die and then raise Him victoriously from the dead?

Hinduism. One of the major concepts of Hinduism is that of *karma,* the law of cause and effect. As a person sows, so shall he or she reap. Bad actions reap suffering and bondage; good actions lead to happiness and well-being. These results are carried from one lifetime to the next. What a person is or experiences in this life is the result of actions in a previous life; the actions of this present life will determine what a person will be and experience in the next life. The law of karma, therefore, explains all the inequalities, injustices, and sufferings of life, even the caste system. Why is a person born intelligent or into a high caste? Why does someone become prosperous in life? It is because of good karma. Why is a person born into a low caste, or is poor? Why does he or she suffer calamity or sorrow in life? It is because of bad karma. Furthermore, Hindus insist that all *must* eat the fruit of their deeds, so there is no place for forgiveness; and no one can pass his or her karma on to someone else, so there is no possibility of vicarious suffering. The innocent cannot suffer for the guilty. If a man suffers, it is a sign he is guilty.

What happens, then, when a Christian evangelist describes the humiliation, physical agony, and mental anguish that Christ suffered in Pilate's judgment hall and on the cross? The immediate reaction of the Hindu listener is, "This Jesus must have been a very wicked man in his previous life in order to suffer so much in this life!" For according to the law of karma, if a person suffers, it is a sign of personal guilt. This, of course, cuts across the whole idea of atonement.

How does the missionary get over this hurdle? It is necessary to point out to Hindu friends that the statement "You reap what you sow" is only a half-truth. Other people also reap what we sow—good or bad. During World War II Adolf Hitler sowed prejudice and hatred, and 6 million innocent Jews died as a result. Louis Pasteur, the French chemist and bacteriologist of the nineteenth century, used his skill and wisdom to develop the technique of immunization against disease, and since then countless millions have benefited from the discovery. We observe all around us that often one person sows and another reaps. If the parents sin, their children and society suffer. If the parents are good, their children and society benefit. Our deeds affect the family, society, and the world.

This fact opens the door to vicariousness. Suppose one man, the most significant person in history, organically connected with the whole world, sowed himself on the cross. Could the whole world reap the benefits? If Jesus were only a man, He could not pass on the benefits to the whole race. His death would be only a martyrdom. But suppose God would sow. Could He pass on the results to all mankind? This is possible! Jesus was the Son of man and the Son of God. He was the God-man—God in human flesh. He deliberately went to the cross and laid down His life. Can we, then, reap what He sowed and not what *we* have sown? If so, this opens up great possibilities—forgiveness, freedom, life!

The law of self-sacrifice runs through life, from the lowest to the very highest of life. In any realm those who save others cannot save themselves from trouble, sorrow, and sometimes even death. The seed gives itself and dies in order to produce a harvest. A mother bird throws herself into the jaws of a serpent in order to save her young. The human mother goes down into the valley of death to bring a child into the world. The young soldier, with all of life before him, takes his own life into his hands and marches out against the enemy's bayonets in order to save home and country. This spirit of sacrifice is the most noble thing in life.

Now if this is a universal law—and it seems to be—then when we come to God, the highest Being, we would expect to find in Him the greatest and noblest expression of sacrificial love in the whole universe. Otherwise, the creature would be greater than the Creator. A worm would be greater, a bird, an animal; they give themselves, but not God! It is unthinkable that God would write a law of saving by sacrifice throughout the universe and be empty of it Himself. If there is not a loving, sacrificing God in the universe, then there ought to be! The highest in humanity and in nature calls for it.

The cross shows that there is such a God. When Jesus was suffering untold agony on the cross, the people mocked Him and said, "He saved others; He cannot save Himself" (Matt. 27:42). Strange as it may seem, the mocking phrase of those hate-crazed enemies became the central truth of Christianity. He was saving others and therefore could not save Himself. Here we see sacrificial love at its highest, for here was the God of the universe sacrificing Himself for lost humanity; the Divine suffering for the human, the innocent for the guilty, the sinless for the sinful.

Does the cross then repeal the law of karma? No. It merely introduces a higher law. In the universe every law is restrained by a higher law. For example, the law of aerodynamics overcomes the law of gravity and enables a plane to fly. In the cross of Christ, God introduces a higher law, the law of sacrificial love, which overcomes the law of karma. If we take hold of that law and let it operate in our lives, we suspend the old law and are lifted above it. We find mercy and pardon. But if we do not take advantage of the higher law, then the lower law of karma comes into operation, and we will reap what we sow.

In this chapter we have sought to explain some of the problems that missionaries on the foreign field face when they attempt to preach the Gospel in a culture other than their own. These difficulties are serious but not insurmountable. Missionaries must master the language, understand the culture, and study the religious concepts of the people if they are to be effective communicators of the truth in Christ Jesus.Jesus. This is an arduous but rewarding task. People on the home front need to understand all these problems and stand behind their missionaries with their sympathy, support, and prayers.

PART FIVE

STRATEGIC MOVEMENTS—What's New in Missions?

Recent movements have had a profound impact on the worldwide mission of the church. The Church Growth movement, under the leadership of Dr. Donald McGavran, has called the church back to its primary task of evangelism and church planting. Through a wise use of cultural anthropology it has given us the skills to understand what makes churches grow and what prevents them from growing. Today, centers of Church Growth have been established in many countries and seminars are being held on a wide scale.

There is a strong conviction that the Western missionary movement has dwindled down to mere interchurch aid. The majority of our missionaries are serving existing churches. We need to get back to pioneer or frontier missions and concentrate on reaching the hidden peoples of the world who are not in contact with any Christian churches. In this endeavor the growing number of new Third World missions is playing an increasingly significant role. Churches around the world are engaged in a new partnership for world mission.

TWELVE

CHURCH GROWTH

One of the most significant and far-reaching movements of the past two decades is that which is commonly known as the Church Growth movement. It has produced a vast amount of research and literature, raised up a whole new breed of missiologists, and brought into existence a number of departments and schools of world mission across the world. Representing a radically new approach to mission, it has produced a revolution in missionary strategy in our day. Without doubt the movement will continue to influence missionary thinking for many years to come.

The man whose name has been most widely linked with the Church Growth movement is Dr. Donald McGavran, a thirty-year veteran of missionary service in India. He began forming his pioneering ideas of the dynamics of church growth as early as the 1930s, when he was secretary-treasurer of his mission. Disturbed by the large sums of money the mission spent and the relatively small number of converts the mission won to Christ, McGavran began searching for ways for the investment of money and personnel to yield greater dividends for Christ. He carefully studied India's "people movements," in which large numbers of outcaste people were won to Christ, to find answers to the question of how churches grow. In this search he was greatly influenced by the Reverend (later Bishop) J. Waskom Pickett of the Methodist Church and his survey, *Christian Mass Move-*

ments in India. The results of McGavran's studies were published in 1955 in *The Bridges of God: A Study in the Strategy of Missions* and then four years later in a companion volume entitled *How Churches Grow.*

Feeling the need for additional research, Dr. McGavran traveled extensively for a few years, and then in 1961 moved to Eugene, Oregon to open the Institute for Church Growth on the campus of Northwest Christian College. There he was joined by Dr. Alan Tippett from Australia, an anthropologist and former Methodist missionary to the Fiji Islands. These two men forged the basic principles of the Church Growth school of thought and gave the movement its original impetus. In 1965 they moved to Fuller Theological Seminary in Pasadena, California and established the School of World Mission, which now has about eight or nine distinguished members on its faculty. In 1970 Dr. McGavran published his classic book *Understanding Church Growth,* which reflects his mature thinking on the subject and is now accepted as the standard text for church growth in seminaries and Bible schools. (The book was revised in 1980.) Dr. McGavran is now retired but still exerts a powerful influence on the entire movement.

The Theology of Church Growth

Church growth is defined as an increase in the number of baptized believers and in the number of worshiping congregations. The term does not exclude growth in faith and knowledge (that is, the perfecting of believers), but it does emphasize numerical growth as a sign of, and an aid to, internal growth. Only a church that is alive can grow, and when a church grows it becomes more alive. The multiplication of churches, therefore, is "a chief and irreplaceable purpose of the Church"; not the *only* purpose, but certainly an *indispensible* purpose of the church's mission (Donald McGavran, *Understanding Church Growth,* Eerdmans, p. 24). Our task is to proclaim the good news of Jesus Christ with a view to persuading men and women to become His disciples and responsible members of His church. Our task is to help existing churches grow and to establish churches where there are no churches.

Church growth, its advocates insist, is theologically required. God wants church growth; it is His will. He desires to reconcile the people of the world to Himself through Jesus Christ and to incorporate them into the fellowship of His church. So church growth is a test of the church's faithfulness. The motive is not self-aggrandizement, but obedience to the will of God.

The Bible pictures God as the one who finds. This is clearly seen in the parables of Jesus. The woman does not only search, she searches *until she finds* the lost coin. The shepherd does not make a token hunt and return empty-handed. He goes after the lost sheep *until he finds* it. Searching is not the purpose; finding is. God is not pleased with a token search. He wants lost people found.

God is interested in results. Proclamation is always for a verdict. Jesus said not only, *"preach* the Gospel," but also *"disciple* all nations." Mission in the New Testament was never proclamation for proclamation's sake; it was proclamation in order to bring people to salvation. Witness was never simply discharging a duty—an end in itself. It was a witness that people might believe. Indifference to results is the opposite of biblical mission.

God desires multitudes to be found. It is not His will that any should perish. Some, of course, do perish, but that is not His will. Jesus commanded that we disciple "all nations," meaning all peoples. That is more than the winning of a few scattered individuals. It was after the disciples had caught "a multitude of fish" that Jesus called them to be "fishers of men." This suggests that they would catch a multitude of men. The Book of Acts is a record of multitudes coming into the church. Note the following verses that refer to the fantastic growth of the early church:

> All these with one accord devoted themselves to prayer. The company of persons was in all about a hundred and twenty. (Acts 1:14-15)
>
> Those who received his word were baptized, and there were added that day about three thousand souls. (Acts 2:41)
>
> But many of those who heard the word believed; and

the number of the men came to about five thousand. (Acts 4:4)

And more than ever believers were added to the Lord, multitudes both of men and women. (Acts 5:14)

And the word of God increased; and the number of the disciples multiplied greatly in Jerusalem, and a great many of the priests were obedient to the faith. (Acts 6:7)

Philip went down to a city of Samaria and proclaimed to them the Christ. And the multitudes with one accord gave heed to what was said by Philip. (Acts 8:5-6)

So the church throughout all Judea, Galilee and Samaria had peace and was built up; and walking in the fear of the Lord and in the comfort of the Holy Spirit, it was multiplied. (Acts 9:31)

And the hand of the Lord was with them, and a great number that believed turned to the Lord. (Acts 11:21)

So the churches were strengthened in the faith, and they increased in numbers daily. (Acts 16:5)

And they said to him, "You see, brother, how many thousands there are among the Jews who have believed." (Acts 21:20)

Notice in these verses such words and phrases as *multitudes, a great many, increased, multiplied.* Also take note that not only were new disciples added to existing churches, but the number of churches multiplied. Thus church growth is firmly rooted in the New Testament.

The motive for the salvation of multitudes and the expansion of the church is found in 2 Corinthians 4:15—"so that as grace extends to more and more people it may increase thanksgiving, to the glory of God."

The Mosaic of Society
Church growth is rooted in theology. We are interested in it because God is interested in it. But at the same time, church growth takes place along sociological and cultural lines. The social structure is the soil in which the church must be planted. Society is made up of various patterns and conditions that put their stamp upon a people in a hundred different ways—for example, their attitudes toward leisure,

work, God, worship, sex, marriage, and the world.

Advocates of church growth believe strongly that the study of society and the social structure of a people is essential to church growth. Ignorance of and indifference to the social structure may be a serious hindrance to missionary work. They, therefore, urge the use of the principles of sociology and anthropology. The more we know about how people organize their lives, how they think, make innovations, and shift to new ideas, the better we can help them make the transition to the Christian faith. By themselves, these sciences are neutral. They neither favor nor oppose the expansion of the Christian religion. They are bodies of knowledge about how people behave. This knowledge should be yoked to the missionary passion and used for the glory of God and the expansion of His church.

One of the most important concepts that Dr. McGavran gleaned from the behavioral sciences was that which he chose to call the "mosaic of society." By this he means that any given society is made up of a number of subsocieties or subcultures. Society is not a uniform wall with one color of paint; it is rather a mosaic of different colors and patterns. It consists of many "homogeneous units" in which the members have one or more characteristics in common and feel an identity of their own. The members of each unit have a certain people-consciousness and refer to themselves as "we" as opposed to "they," members of other groups.

There are several types of these homogeneous units, which make up the mosaic of a given country. There are *ethnic* groupings, such as (in the U.S.A.) whites, blacks, native Americans, Latin Americans, Chinese, Japanese, Arabs, etc. Some of these can be broken down into further divisions. For example, among the whites there are the English, Scots, Irish, Germans, Italians, French, and Poles. Then there are the *linguistic* homogeneous units, which usually coincide with the ethnic backgrounds: those who speak English, Spanish, French, Arabic, Korean, and a host of other languages spoken by first generation immigrants. *Religion* is still another factor: Christian (Roman Catholic and Protestant), Muslim, Hindu, Buddhist, Animist (the native American tribes), and secular humanists. Under the umbrella of *socioeconomic factors*, there is a great variety of homogeneous units, such as rich, middle-class, and poor; senior citizens, middle-aged, and youth; educated and illiterate; management, labor, blue-collar, white-collar; urban, suburban, and rural. Finally, there are the *geographical* units of the mosaic: New England, the South, Southwest, Midwest, the Bible Belt.

The "mosaic of society" has significant implications for the mission of the church. In the first place, since each has its own characteristics and sense of identity, each unit will require a special approach or strategy of evangelism. The way we approach a migratory tribe in Africa that is constantly on the move will be different from the way we approach a people who remain in one spot all their lives. There will have to be different strategies for reaching high-caste Brahmins and low-caste Madigas in India; different strategies for Muslims and Hindus; different strategies for illiterate hill tribes and sophisticated city dwellers. The message will be essentially the same in each case, but the form in which it is presented will vary with the cultural and religious background of the people.

Then again, since each group has its own characteristics and sense of identity, each unit will produce a different type of Christianity, suited to its own customs and cultural patterns. The type of music, patterns of worship, style of preaching, form of art and architecture, kinds of offerings—just to mention a few items—will vary from group to group. We must not expect every group to express their Christian faith in the same way. There is a blessed unity that binds together Christians of all nations—one Lord, one Spirit, one faith, one baptism—but unity doesn't necessarily mean uniformity in all outer forms. The variety of Christian expression is just as beautiful as the unity of Christian experience. Some Christians will take their shoes off and sit on the floor in their houses of worship; others will keep their shoes on and sit on benches. Some Christians will clap their hands or play cymbals when they sing; others will raise their hands in the air. Some Christians will use piano and organ to accompany their music; others will use flute, drum, and castanets; still others will use guitar. Some will present their offerings in check or cash; others will bring grain, fruit, or vegetables. Some Christians will take Communion with grape juice and wafer; others will use a sweet potato and wild berry juice. Some Christian preachers will preach with fire and emotion; others will preach in a conversational tone with few gestures. The important thing is for Christians to recognize the differences in culture and allow fellow Christians to worship and live out the Christian life in ways that are familiar and comfortable to them. One group should not seek to impose its ways and forms upon every other group, with the belief that its culture is the best or only one there is.

Receptivity of Groups

Another very significant facet of the social mosaic is that each homogeneous unit "ripens" at a different time and differs in its degree of receptivity (or hostility) to the Gospel. Some groups are open to the Gospel, some are indifferent, others are opposed. Jesus recognized this fact in His Parable of the Sower, when He talked about differences in the soil: shallow, rocky, thorny, and fertile ground. He found some groups receptive to His message (as the publicans and sinners), and others hostile (like the Pharisees and members of the Sanhedrin). Jesus warned the disciples when He sent them out to preach that some would receive and others would reject them.

Some groups or areas may be hostile to the Christian message at one time and then later become receptive. In such cases Christian workers have to be satisfied with plowing the ground, sowing the seed, and watering the earth, with the hope that one day the ground will become fertile and produce a harvest. Other groups or areas may be receptive today, but could become hostile later on. In these situations, Christian workers should reap the harvest while it is ripe, or it may be too late.

Thus, one of the major principles of the Church Growth movement is that the church must concentrate its money and personnel on receptive groups. This does not mean that we should neglect or abandon difficult areas; we always need a Christian presence to continue sowing the seed in these hard places, hoping for brighter days ahead. But it just makes good sense to put in the sickle where the harvest is ripe, or the grain may rot in the field. Church growth advocates are critical of the equalitarian approach to mission—treating every section of the work as equal, in order not to offend the feelings of missionaries. This attitude says in advance that it will pay no attention to differing responses and to the growth of the church.

It is at this point that the social sciences can again be of value to mission boards. A study of the patterns of a society will help missionaries to see where groups of people are ripe for the Gospel and will therefore offer the greatest response to its proclamation. Research has shown that such factors as dissatisfaction or unrest, reaction to the old culture system, political and economic upheaval, and migrations of people produce an attitude of openness to the Christian message. On the other hand, such factors as self-satisfaction, bondage to tradition, and danger to one's economic privileges all tend to foster a certain resistance to the Gospel, which is looked on as a threat to the status quo.

From the beginning, Dr. McGavran and his colleagues have vigorously contended that there are more winnable people in the world today than ever before and that the church worldwide should pool its resources to win these people for Christ. Fantastic church growth is possible in many areas of the world. Where the church can grow, it ought to grow. Dr. McGavran recognizes that there are difficult fields where we can expect but little church growth. But he is concerned about the church making the difficulty of some areas the norm for all areas; he is concerned about the church developing a mentality of expecting little. He is suspicious of those who glibly say, "We are interested in quality, not quantity." It is his belief that there are many fruitful areas where the church is failing to reap a harvest because of the wrong approach to church growth.

The Homogeneous Unit Principle

Perhaps the most controversial concept of the Church Growth movement is the one called the "homogeneous unit principle." Briefly, it is summed up in Dr. McGavran's much quoted axiom: "People like to become Christians without crossing racial, linguistic, or class barriers." Notice that he says people *like* to, not *ought* to.

This statement is based on the observation that people like to be with, and have fellowship with, other members of their own group. As the old saying goes, "Birds of a feather flock together." People feel more comfortable and at home with those who come from the same background, speak the same language, and follow the same customs. This is a statement of fact, a description of how human beings behave.

When we look around, we notice that congregations and denominations are generally formed along cultural and homogeneous lines. In this country, blacks like to worship together because they enjoy a particular style of music and preaching and are not bound by the clock. Whites enjoy worshiping together because they are used to a more formal ritual and like a preacher who "quits on time." The mainline denominations are usually made up of middle-class economic groups, while Pentecostal churches tend to attract the lower economic groups. When we look at churches across the seas, we find that a majority of congregations follow ethnic, caste, or tribal lines. The Christian faith seems to flow more easily within each piece of the mosaic. People tend to resist the Gospel if they feel that by becoming Christians they have to adopt a foreign culture and can no longer be themselves.

A further observation is that homogeneous congregations, both at home and abroad, seem to grow more rapidly than heterogeneous congregations—those that are composed of people of various backgrounds. Not that all single-unit congregations are growing, nor that no mixed congregation is growing, but as a general rule, the former grows faster than the latter.

Based on these facts, proponents of the Church Growth movement advocate that we should encourage the formation and multiplication of churches within the various segments of the social mosaic. We should recognize the diversity of cultures and grant each group the liberty to maintain its own culture. As an evangelistic tool, this will enhance church growth and hasten the evangelization of the world. Of course, when people become disciples of Christ, there are some things they are going to have to give up; there are certain aspects of their culture that will have to be purged. But there are also values in every culture that need to be preserved and can be used for the good of the church and the glory of God.

Church Growth leaders are quick to point out that no congregation should be exclusive, seeking to exist for only one group. The door of the church should be open to all. Every person, regardless of race, color, class, or caste should be welcomed into the fellowship. But at the same time, no congregation can insist that everyone join their ranks and become like them. Members of each group should have the privilege of forming their own congregations and maintaining their own identity. This principle was followed in the early church, when the council at Jerusalem decided that Gentiles entering the church need not become Jewish Christians (follow Jewish diet and customs) but could be Gentile Christians and remain in their own cultural framework.

The homogeneous unit principle has been fiercely contested by many church leaders. They argue that it is a subtle form of segregation, maintaining old racial and cultural prejudices. Surely, they contend, the Gospel has power to save people from their biases and to unite them in the fellowship of the church. After all, Christ came to break down the old barriers between Jew and Gentile, slave and free, male and female. It may be that people like to stick to their own kind, but isn't that a symptom of human sinfulness? Some also argue that mixed congregations are stronger in their Christian witness than homogeneous churches. The more mixed the congregation is, especially in class and color, the greater its opportunity to demonstrate the power of Christ.

McGavran's answer to these critics is that Christian unity is certainly a basic principle of the Christian faith. All Christians should live together harmoniously. But that can happen only through the power of the Holy Spirit working in Christians. Unity is the fruit of the Spirit, and not a prerequisite for baptism. People must first become Christians, then the Holy Spirit works. We can't expect unity from non-Christians.

The point is to find ways and means for Christian brotherhood to be enjoyed to the greatest possible extent, while at the same time maintaining a high evangelistic potential.

Personally, I feel there is validity to the homogeneous unit principle, but there is a danger of pushing it too far. Certainly, when a difference in language is involved, the only practical thing is to have separate congregations. Koreans and Spanish-speaking people should not be expected to join English-speaking congregations. They will want to sing, read the Scriptures, and hear the Gospel preached in their own mother tongue. In some cases, when people come from vastly different cultural backgrounds, it may be the wisest policy to develop congregations along cultural lines. For example, converts from Islam often feel very much out of place worshiping with converts from Hinduism. Their name for God, postures in prayer, style of music, and worship forms are all so different from those of Hindu converts. Muslims are more likely to become Christians and join the church if they feel they can form their own congregations and follow their own cultural patterns. In compact neighborhoods where members of one particular ethnic background are living together, they will naturally form homogeneous congregations—as do Chinese in Chinatown, and Hispanics in "little Cuba."

The homogeneous unit principle, however, should not be pushed to extremes, such as putting all the poor people into one church and all the rich into another or separating "charismatics" from "noncharismatics." In neighborhoods where people from different ethnic and cultural backgrounds are already living together harmoniously, it would be ridiculous to try to form separate congregations for the various segments. It would be most natural for all residents of the neighborhood to worship together in one congregation. Besides, it is always possible to have homogeneous groups within a mixed congregation, such as singles, senior citizens, youth, women, and professionals. Thus, the homogeneous unit principle has its merits but also its limitations. In certain cases it is legitimate; in others harmful. Much depends on the situation.

People Movements

The last important aspect of the Church Growth movement is that of people movements. Such movements are possible among tight-knit ethnic societies, such as tribes, clans, or castes, where there is a strong group consciousness and where marriage and intimate life take place only within the society.

In Western societies we take pride in our individualism. Individuals have the liberty to make their own major decisions of life, such as selecting a husband or wife, choosing an occupation, and making a religious decision. In the area of religion, an individual may go off to a Billy Graham crusade or a church revival somewhere, and when the invitation is given, go down to the front and make "a decision for Christ." That person then goes home and announces to the rest of the family, "I have surrendered my life to Jesus Christ. I am going to follow Him." That decision does not usually mean that the individual has to turn his back on his or her former religion and culture and enter a whole new society. Often the person was already a Christian in name before; now he or she has become a born-again Christian. And since Christianity is the religion of the majority, no major social upheaval is involved. Individual conversion in Western countries is acknowledged as the common way to come to Christ, and it is a good way.

But in most Afro-Asian societies, individualism is not the way of life. It is not the individual, but the group that is all-important. The group may be the extended family, the tribe, or the caste. And the decision-making machinery is different. Such important decisions as occupation, marriage, and religion are made in consultation with the group, not by the individual.

So a problem arises when a missionary who comes from a highly individualistic society enters a close-knit non-Christian society and seeks to make individual conversions. What happens when a person goes back to his or her family and people and announces, "I have been baptized as a Christian"? The group feels that the individual has committed a highly antisocial act, has in fact become a rebel. For the first time, the person has made a major decision all alone, without consulting the group. The individual is thrown out of the family and group and suffers "social dislocation." Contact with the group is severed, and any further possibility of witnessing for Christ to one's own people is cut off. Usually the missionary feels responsible for such spiritual orphans and gathers them together on the mission compound for shelter and nurture. The whole process puts the group against the church and the church against the group. Christians are looked on as kidnappers. The group is antagonistic to the missionary, the Gospel, and the individual convert.

Church Growth strategists assert that in working among people of such close-knit societies, missionaries should take a group approach, rather than an individualistic approach. When the first few individuals begin to claim faith in Jesus Christ, missionaries should not be in a rush to baptize them immediately. They should urge these new believers to go back home, share their faith with their families, and talk matters over with the elders. The believers should urge the group to discuss the pros and cons of this new faith among themselves, as they sit at meals and around the campfire. In other words, the normal decision-making process should be allowed to operate. Then when entire families come to faith in Christ as the Saviour, a whole new pattern is established. The group has been consulted. To become a Christian is no longer an antisocial act. If, after all attempts, the family does not come, then the individual's conscience is free. He can say, "I tried my best; I have exhausted all the possibilities to win my family members." The people can also say, "Yes, he tried his best; we don't want to become Christians; it's our decision."

Results of the group approach are just the opposite of the individualistic approach. When whole families come into the church together, no social dislocation takes place. Converts don't go off to live on the mission compound. They stay on in their homes and occupations. Contact with the group is maintained, and the door to further witness and outreach is kept open. More and more families, over the years, come into the Christian faith and the church, and soon a people movement is on the way.

People movements have not only a quantitative, but also a qualitative difference about them. When a large number of families enter the church, they bring their social structures and patterns of leadership with them. People-movement churches tend to be far more indigenous than congregations made up of scattered individuals who have been ostracized from their community. The Gospel has a chance to work, not only in the lives of individuals, but in their whole cultural system as well. Then again, discipline in the newly formed churches is much more effective, because it is not the missionaries imposing regulations from the outside, but the group leaders endeavoring to maintain Christian standards from within. The pressure of the group helps keep the individual from going astray. Furthermore, people movements are much more stable, simply because in union there is strength, and a large group of converts can stand up under persecution much better than a few individuals.

It must be made clear that a people movement is not merely a large *number* of people coming to Christ at one time. When 1,500 persons come forward in a Billy Graham meeting to accept Christ, that is not a people movement. It is merely so many individuals, unrelated to each other, making decisions separately for Christ. Neither is a people movement wholesale acceptance into the church without Christian experience or understanding; it does not mean careless accession, promiscuous baptism, or neglect of quality.

Dr. McGavran says that people movements are based on "multi-individual, mutually interdependent action." It is not a group decision, for a group does not have a mind. Only an individual can make a decision. The people movement is several people, closely knit together in society, making a decision with mutual consultation. The decision may take several months of discussion. Usually the entire group does not come to Christ, but only a portion. But once a people movement is initiated, often individuals start coming; by then it is possible and safe, because the group has decided it is all right for a person to become a Christian. It may take several years before the whole tribe or caste comes to faith in Christ.

A casual study of mission history will reveal that a large majority of the first generation converts in Asia and Africa came into the church through people movements. These group movements have produced some of the strongest Christian churches to be found anywhere in the world. For example, there is the great Batak Church of Sumatra, Indonesia, numbering over a million members. There is the Karen Church of Burma with over 600,000 members. We can also mention the numerous churches that have come out of the Madiga caste in south India, the hill tribes of northeast India, or the tribal peoples of the South Pacific islands. If one were to discount the results of people movements around the world, there wouldn't be many Christians left. So the group approach has proved to be God's way of reaching the multitudes in the past, and will continue to be an effective method in other parts of the world in the future.

In the beginning the Church Growth movement related primarily to mission strategy across the seas. But it soon became evident that many of these same principles could and should be applied to the church at home. An increasing concern for church growth in the North American scene was evident. Mainline denominations continued to show a decline in membership, while at the same time the population and number of unchurched people were increasing. Thus, a few years ago the Institute for American Church Growth was established under the leadership of Win Arn, with headquarters at Pasadena, California. Much research has been done on the question of why American churches grow or do not grow. Several helpful books have come off the press, written by such persons as Peter Wagner, Lyle Schaller, Vergil Gerber, and Win Arn.

Such attitudes as indifference to evangelism, satisfaction with the status quo, lack of involvement of the laity, and ignorance of the social context are prime reasons for the lack of growth in many churches. On the other hand, establishing biblical priorities, setting goals, and developing the necessary resources to reach those goals are some of the necessary ingredients for a growing church. Seminars and workshops on church growth are being held in many centers these days, and also in individual congregations. A few denominations have officially adopted church growth principles as a policy for the entire membership.

Without doubt the church around the world is indebted to the Church Growth movement for·calling it back to its primary mission of world evangelization and giving it the skills to fulfill its goal.

THIRTEEN

FRONTIER MISSIONS

Much has been accomplished! Much remains to be done! This sums up the present status of the world mission of the church.

We are grateful to God for all that has been achieved through His witnesses around the world during the past 175 years or more. With a few exceptions, the church of Jesus Christ has been established in almost every part of the world. Christians are everywhere—on every continent, in practically every nation, on every island of the sea.

In some areas the followers of Jesus Christ are but a tiny minority. In Japan, for example, Christians make up only about 1 percent of the total population. In Thailand and Bangladesh they make up only a fraction of 1 percent, while in Nepal they are merely a handful. In North Africa and most of the Middle East countries, there are only small numbers of Christians from the Berber and Arab populations. And yet we thank God for the faithful few who are bearing witness to His name in these countries and for the tiny ray of light shining in the darkness.

In other areas the church has experienced spectacular growth in the past several decades. In Korea, for example, the number of Christians has doubled every ten years since 1940. It has gone from only 300,000 to over 11 million (25 percent of the population) today. On an average, six and one-half new congregations are established every day in

Korea. There are over 4,000 churches in the capital city alone. About 50 percent of the army is Christian. The Central Assembly of God Church in Seoul is the largest congregation in the world with over 500,000 members. Their new sanctuary, which accommodates about 25,000 people, is packed out six times on a Sunday. The largest Presbyterian church (45,000 members) and largest Methodist church (18,000) are in Korea. The latter grew by 14,000 in the past four years. Korean churches are now sending missionaries and giving financial help to churches overseas.

Since the aborted Communist coup in Indonesia in September 1965, the number of Christians has doubled in that land, now standing at approximately 17 million (11 percent of the population). A great revival has swept the church in many parts of the archipelago. More Muslims have been won to Christ in Indonesia than in all of the rest of the Islamic world.

The growth of the church in Africa is indeed a modern miracle. In 1900 there were only 10 million Christians on the continent; today there are 203 million (44.2 percent). Six million Christians are being added every year. David Barrett, church statistician, estimates that by the year 2000 there will be 393 million Christians in Africa (59 percent) out of a population of approximately 813 million. He also predicts that Africa will become the center of world Christendom in the next two or three decades.

In Latin America, the evangelical movement has experienced spectacular growth since the turn of the century. In 1900 there were only about 933,000 (1.4 percent) evangelical Christians south of the border. Today there are over 18 million (5 percent). The annual growth is about 10 percent. Three-fourths of all Protestants in Latin America are Pentecostals. One Pentecostal church in Sao Paulo, Brazil can accommodate 25,000 worshipers; another in Santiago, Chile seats 15,000.

The story of mainland China, however, is the greatest miracle of all times. When Communists took over the country in 1949, there were only a million Protestants and three million Roman Catholics in the country. All missionaries were forced to leave and all foreign funds were cut off. All

Christian institutions were taken over by the government. Many churches were closed, and most church leaders were imprisoned. Pastors were sent to work in fields and factories. During the Cultural Revolution—from 1966–1976—the church suffered severe persecution. All church buildings were taken over; all Bible schools and seminaries were closed; nothing was left of the organizational forms of the church. Christians went into hiding but continued to worship secretly in hundreds of house churches across the land. These were led by laypersons, many of them women. The Far East Broadcasting Company from Manila continued to beam the Gospel into China over the air waves, reading choice passages of Scripture at dictation speed, so Christians in China could copy them down in the secrecy of their homes.

So here was a church with no organization, no institutions, no pastors, no buildings, no finances, and very few Bibles. But there were Christian men and women, and there was the Holy Spirit! The Christians witnessed quietly, person to person, loved their enemies, and lived exemplary lives. The Spirit performed miracles of healing and transformation. And now after China has slightly opened its doors to the outside world and we can take a peek in, what have we found? That small band of Christians has grown to somewhere between 35 and 50 *million* believers! It is hard to get exact figures, but many feel the number of Christians is closer to the 50-million mark. We are reminded of the words of Jesus when He said, "Upon this rock I will build My church; and the gates of hell shall not prevail against it" (Matt. 16:18). Certainly the church in China is a classic illustration of the truth of this statement.

At present around the world each day about 65,000 new converts are entering the fellowship of the Christian church. Each week about 1,600 new congregations are formed. Truly the Spirit of God is working in unusual ways. For all this we are sincerely thankful to our sovereign Lord.

The Unfinished Task

In spite of all that we have accomplished, however, the task of world evangelization is far from complete. In fact, because of the universal population explosion, our task is becoming greater and greater all the time. The number of non-Christians around the world doubled between 1900 and 1965 and will triple by the year 2000. This means there are more people to be reached for Christ than ever before in the history of the church.

There are a few countries, such as Saudi Arabia, Afghanistan, and Tibet, where the Christian movement has not penetrated because of fast-closed doors. No national Christians or churches are to be found in these areas. All we can do at present is earnestly pray that God in His sovereign power would somehow make it possible for these nations to be reached with the Gospel. Perhaps a few citizens from these lands will come to Christ while studying or working abroad and then carry the Good News back to their people.

Three major blocks of people around the world are yet to be evangelized: 950 million people in mainland China; over 658 million Hindus in India; and 850 million Muslims in the Islamic world, stretching all the way from Morocco in Northwest Africa, through the Middle East, to Southeast Asia. The world population has just crossed the 5-billion mark, and out of this number roughly 1.5 billion (30 percent) are at least nominally Christian (Protestants, Catholics, and Eastern Orthodox). That means there are 3.5 billion yet to be evangelized.

How do we evangelize 3.5 billion people? It seems like an impossible task, doesn't it?

Dr. Ralph Winter, Director of the U.S. Center for World Mission in Pasadena, California, has offered a very practical solution to this problem. He points out that we cannot evangelize the world by reaching one person at a time. Some people have naively suggested that if every Christian would go out and win one new person to Christ, and that person in turn would win another, and so on, within a few years we could evangelize everyone in the world. But this would be possible only if the Christian witnesses knew the language and culture of the persons to whom they were communicating. The truth of the matter is, however, that there are many language and culture groups throughout the world in which there is not a single Christian. Somebody will have to come from the outside and study their language and culture before he or she can witness to them about Christ. In other words, it will require cross-cultural communication.

Four Types of Evangelism

To make this point clearer, Dr. Winter speaks of four types of evangelism, to which he gives the symbols of E-0, E-1, E-2, and E-3.

E-0 evangelism is taking the Gospel to *nominal Christians in one's own culture.* For example, a born-again Christian witnesses to a fellow church member who does not have a personal relationship with Christ.

E-1 evangelism is taking the Gospel to *non-Christians in one's own culture* or society. An example would be an American who is a committed Christian witnessing to a fellow American who claims to be an atheist and is outside the church; or a Christian convert from Hinduism witnessing to his relatives and friends who are still Hindus. In E-0 and E-1 evangelism, no ethnic, cultural, religious, or linguistic barriers have to be crossed. People are talking to their own kind of people in their own languages. This is simple witnessing and does not require any specialized training. It is the easiest and most powerful type of evangelism.

E-2 and E-3 evangelism are both cross-cultural; barriers of language, culture, and/or religion have to be overcome. This is true missionary work and requires specialized training in cross-cultural communication. It is much more difficult than E-0 and E-1 evangelism. Missionaries must take time to learn the language, understand the customs and worldview, and study the religion of the people to whom they are ministering.

The only difference between E-2 and E-3 evangelism is in the extent of the barriers to be crossed. E-2 evangelism is *taking the Gospel cross-culturally, but within the same family of cultures or languages.* For example, an American Protestant missionary goes to Italy to work among Roman Catholics. He has to learn another language, but Italian and English both come from Latin and use the same alphabet in writing. Both missionary and recipient are Christian, but they belong to different branches of Christendom. Another example of E-2 evangelism would be a white American witnessing to an Arab immigrant in the United States who is Muslim by religion, but speaks English fluently. Only one barrier has to be crossed, that of religion. A third example would be a convert from Hinduism in India witnessing to a Muslim who speaks the same language.

E-3 evangelism is *taking the Gospel cross-culturally to a radically different culture from one's own—the language, ethnic background, and religion are all entirely different.* For example, an American missionary goes to work among the Auca Indians of Colombia, South America. The Aucas are racially different, speak an entirely foreign language, are animists by religion, and have a culture all their own.

It is culture and not geography that makes the difference between the various types of evangelism. One can cross the seas and be engaged only in E-1 evangelism, as an American pastor ministering to a congregation of Americans living in Costa Rica, Central America. On the other hand, one can stay in his own country and yet be engaged in E-3 evangelism, as a white American working among the Navaho Indians in New Mexico.

The Great Commission as recorded in the Book of Acts clearly implies that different types of evangelism are necessary to reach different people groups. Jesus said, "You shall be my witnesses in Jerusalem and in all Judea and Samaria and to the end of the earth" (Acts 1:8). We usually read *geography* into these words and think that Jesus was merely talking about going farther and farther away from where we are. In so doing we miss the true significance of the verse. Jesus was not talking about geographical but *cultural* distance. Witnessing in Jerusalem and Judea is monocultural evangelism—within the same language and culture—where the only barrier to be crossed is the boundary between the Christian community and the world immediately outside. This is what we call "near-neighbor evangelism" (E-1).

Witnessing in Samaria stands for cross-cultural evangelism, involving significant (but not monumental) differences in language and culture (E-2). The Samaritans were racial cousins of the Jews, but had a distinct identity of their own. They spoke a different dialect, followed a few different customs, and worshiped in a different place. Perhaps the greatest barrier was the strong prejudice between Jew and Samaritan.

"To the uttermost part of the earth" involves cross-cultural evangelism of a radical nature, where the people to be reached live, work, talk, and think in languages and cultural patterns utterly different from those of the evangelist (E-3).

Dr. Winter points out that it will take E-2 and E-3 evangelism to reach at least half of the world's population with the Gospel. He divides the people of the world into four major groups: the truly *committed Christians,* who are capable of sharing their faith with others and leading them to Christ— roughly 300 million or 20 percent of the total Christian population; the *nominal Christians*, who lack a personal experience with Christ (1.2 billion); *near-neighbor non-Christians* who have Christians within their cultural group who speak their language and Christian churches nearby that they could join (1 billion); *distant non-Christians*, in whose society there are no Christians or churches (2.5 billion). The nominal Christians can be reached with E-0 evangelism, and the near-neighbor non-Christians with E-1 evangelism; but it will require E-2 or E-3 evangelism to reach the rest. Thus, half the world can be reached with ordinary witnessing, but the other half can be evangelized only by genuine missionary endeavor.

Unreached Peoples

Dr. Ralph Winter also contends that the object of our missionary endeavor should not be merely countries or sovereign states but people groups. Many Christians think that because the Gospel has now gone to the ends of the earth and there are Christians in almost every country, our missionary task is complete. Far from it! Looking at each country as a mosaic of different ethnic, linguistic, and cultural subsocieties, we find that there are hundreds of people groups around the world into which the Gospel has not yet penetrated. These are the "hidden" or "unreached" peoples of the world. For example, there are approximately 23 million Christians in India, the majority of whom are converts from Hinduism. But they represent only about 50 out of 500 or more castes in Hindu society. The remaining castes are virtually untouched by the Gospel. There are 75–80 million

Muslims in India, speaking many languages, who are yet to be evangelized. The same thing is true of the Sikh and Parsee communities and the followers of Buddhism. In addition, approximately 35 million tribal people in India are waiting to hear the Good News of Jesus Christ. This sort of situation can be repeated in country after country.

Evangelizing 3.5 billion persons throughout the world looks like an impossible task. Ralph Winter suggests that we concentrate on reaching people groups instead of individuals, which makes our task more manageable. He estimates that there are roughly 17,000 such unreached groups across the world. Some groups may number only a few hundred; others run into the thousands and even a million or more. The average group is only about 135,000 people. The Missions Advanced Research and Communication Center, a ministry of World Vision International, based in Monrovia, California, has put out a volume each year since 1979, entitled *Unreached Peoples,* which locates and describes a number of these people groups in various countries. Mission boards are urged to prayerfully select and plan to enter one or more of these unreached areas.

The master plan of world evangelization is first for special E-2 and E-3 missionaries to cross cultural barriers into new communities and to establish strong, indigenous churches and then for the national Christians to carry the work forward on the high-powered E-1 level. Thus it is not necessary for the foreign missionary to evangelize the whole area but simply to initiate the movement and establish a church that is able to reproduce itself. When the Christian community reaches about 15–20 percent of the population, then the mission can consider the group a reached people and can move on to new areas. But our task is not complete until we have a vital Christian church among every people group of the world.

The tragedy with our present missionary movement is that most North American missionaries (about 90 percent) are working among people who are already Christians in the Third World. They are attempting to strengthen existing churches and to win nominal Christians to real faith in the Lord. Very few missionaries (10 percent) are endeavoring to evangelize unreached people groups. Thus missions, for the West at least, have dwindled to mere interchurch aid. We need to shift gears and get back to pioneer or frontier missions.

Dr. Winter suggests that the Christian church worldwide recruit an additional 68,000 missionaries (or 34,000 couples) to evangelize the 17,000 unreached people groups around the world. This would mean four missionaries (or two couples) to each group. North American churches with their greater resources could send 40,000 new missionaries out of the total number, and Third World churches an additional 28,000.

How much would this cost? Even if only one-fourth of the 300 million evangelical Christians in the world would get involved, it would mean only 4¢ per person per day!

Evangelizing the world seems like a big task. It is! But it is also a possible and exciting task. For the first time in history it is possible for a church to exist within the language and socialsocial structure of every people group on earth, and it can be done by the year 2000.

THIRD WORLD MISSIONS

One of the fastest growing areas in missions today is the non-Western missionary movement. Until quite recently missionaries, bearers of the Good News, were white men and women from the North Atlantic, Western cultures, a large percentage of them speaking English. But nowadays missionaries come in all colors—black, brown, red, yellow, and white—and speak a great number of languages. It is estimated that at the present time over 15,000 Third World missionaries are engaged in cross-cultural evangelism. This is a clear sign that the churches of Africa, Asia, and Latin America have matured in their spiritual development. They are not merely the objects of missionary activity; they are also agents of mission. They are no longer only receiving bodies, but sending bodies as well. From mission churches they have become missionary churches.

A Story of Growth

Though Third World churches as a whole have not been missionary-sending agencies until quite recently, there have been a few significant exceptions to the rule. In the 1830s a few Jamaican Christians, led by Joseph Merrick, pioneered a missionary movement to the Cameroons. By 1884, Methodist missionaries were going out from India to Malaysia. In 1903, the India Missionary Society was established to evangelize other cultures within the country. Korean Presbyterians began sending missionaries in 1907, among the first being Kee Pung Lee.

The best example of early Third World missions is to be found in the islands of the Pacific. In the 1820s, missionaries like Josua Mateinaniu were hopping from one island to another. Eight Tahitian missionaries preached Christ among heathen villagers on Samoa islands. Five years later the first European missionary arrived to find 2,000 Samoan Christians meeting in small groups in sixty-five villages. Interesting to note is that these islanders were missionaries ten years before David Livingstone landed in Africa and before Hudson Taylor was even born. Later, Christians from Fiji islands sailed to the Solomon islands and proclaimed the Gospel to people there. Altogether, over 1,000 Pacific islanders went out as missionaries to add a remarkable record to the history of Christian expansion. In the chapel of the Theological Seminary in Suva, Fiji there is a list of all these island missionaries, many of whom were killed and eaten by cannibals. Because of the faithfulness of these pioneer evangelists, Oceania is almost entirely Christian today.

One of the most significant missions in the South Pacific was a dynamic society called the Melanesian Brotherhood, organized in 1925 by Ini Kopuria of Guadalcanal with encouragement by both Western missionaries and island Christians. The primary thrust of this society was not to work among Christians, but "to proclaim the teaching of Jesus Christ among the heathen." Each brother was to take a vow not to marry for a year, nor take any salary, nor disobey his superiors. He could choose to renew his vow at the end of each year. Ini, who had been deeply impressed with the life of St. Francis of Assisi, took a lifelong vow in the presence of three bishops. He was joined by six others, and they banded together to go out and preach the Gospel, first to their fellow islanders and then to the regions beyond.

The annals of the Melanesian Brotherhood constitute some of the most famous in missionary history. The Brotherhood eventually divided into households of eight to twelve people throughout the islands. Dressed very simply in black loincloth and white sash, they traveled barefoot throughout the lands. As they grew in numbers, the Brotherhood began to reach out to additional islands: Mala, Santa Cruz, New Britain, and even Papua New Guinea. Over 100 missionaries were sent out in the fifteen years of existence before the disruptive Second World War. Massive bombing and foreign occupation stifled their growth for a season, but not their evangelistic zeal. After the war, between 1955 and 1975, they were successful in winning forty-five villages to Christ in New Britain and New Guinea, involving 9,500 people.

All these heroic efforts in the Third World, however, constituted a mere trickle in the worldwide missionary stream until the decade of the sixties. Then exciting things began to happen. One missionary society after another began to emerge, in country after country. A survey in 1972 revealed at least 203 Protestant and independent missionary societies, sending out at least 3,400 missionaries. Here was a formidable force of missionary personnel daily involved in evangelistic endeavors that had been previously ignored.

Eight years later (1980) careful research found 368 active mission agencies in the Third World, representing an 81 percent increase in this brief period of time. Asia and Oceania together increased 92.6 percent; Latin America decreased by 8 percent. In Africa the number of missionary-sending countries doubled, largely due to the expanding independent church movement. At the same time the number of missionaries in the Third World during this eight-year period increased dramatically from 3,400 to over 13,000, a growth of 282 percent. Both figures include about 460 missionaries from ethnic churches in the U.S.A. and New Zealand. Regionally Asia increased from 1,063 to 4,980 missionaries; Africa, from 1,007 to 5,884; Latin America, from 820 to 952; Oceania, from 61 to 706.

In 1980 the Third World country with the largest number of missionaries was Nigeria in Africa, with 2,500, followed by India with 2,277. The largest mission agency was the Aldura in Nigeria, with 1,250 missionaries, followed by the Burmese Baptist Convention in Burma, with 885 missionaries.

Characteristics of Third World Missions
Many Third World missionaries are working within their own countries, but are reaching out to unevangelized areas

in genuine cross-cultural evangelism. In Nigeria, for example, Christians from the south are penetrating into Muslim communities in the north. The same is true in India, where Christianity is relatively strong in the south but weak and scattered in the north. The Friends Missionary Prayer Band, organized in 1967 by Dr. Samuel Kamalesan and some friends, at present has about 250 missionaries working among tribal peoples in north India. Their goal is to recruit a minimum of 440 missionaries, two for each of the 220 political districts in the northern states. They already have 3,500 converts and have established 150 new congregations.

Kalimantan (formerly known as Borneo) is a rugged island in the Indonesian archipelago, with many mountain chains and coastal swamps. Transportation is exceedingly difficult. The Christian and Missionary Alliance has evangelized many of the Dyak tribal people and organized them into the Kingmi Church. The Kerayan Valley in northeast Kalimantan has a population of 8,000 to 9,000 people, all professing Christians. The Bible school there has an enrollment of 250 students, and every church has four to five pastors. In April 1973, this church established its own mission agency in order to reach additional Dyak tribes in remote areas of the island. With transportation provided by Mission Aviation Fellowship, a Western service organization, between 1973 and 1976 the Kerayan Church sent approximately 40 missionaries to the Berau area (two hours flying time) to the south. The missionaries went for a minimum of two years and ministered to a different tribe in an entirely different language. They planted 25 new churches in the area during that period.

In some cases Third World churches are actually sending missionaries across the seas or to other countries on the same continent (as in Africa). Thus, we find Korean and Singaporean missionaries serving in Thailand, Indonesia, and Malaysia. The same Kingmi Mission in Kalimantan mentioned earlier is now launching an ambitious program to send missionaries to the densely populated island of Java. The mission hopes to establish 500 churches and worshiping groups in Java by 1990. The International Missionary Fellowship, an indigenous Jamaican mission organized in 1962, has trained and sent forth over 35 missionaries to work as partners with various mission societies in India, Indonesia, Papua New Guinea, Nigeria, Bolivia, and Suriname.

High in Bolivia's Andes Mountains is a large tribe of Aymara Indians, numbering over 1 million. For a long time they were resistant to the Gospel, but during the 1970s a group movement developed and within five years 380 new congregations were established. The evangelistic activity was carried on primarily by the Aymaras themselves. In response to a recent challenge, the Bolivian Aymaras have now agreed to send two couples to work among the Navaho in New Mexico in the United States. One of the Aymara church leaders commented, saying, "For us to send missionaries to the Navaho Indians is equivalent to the Americans sending a man to the moon!" It will be a difficult and complex assignment, but there are several advantages. Though their languages are totally different, cultural similarities are abundant. Both Aymara and Navaho Indians are similar in their physical features, environment, lifestyles, religious idolatry, and historical background under the Spanish. Furthermore, Aymaras do not have the historical disadvantages that white American missionaries have. Relationships will be much more favorable.

An interesting feature of Third World mission societies is that they are self-supporting and operate their own training centers. They will not accept foreign funds to pay mission salaries; they believe strongly that the national Christians must accept this responsibility. When people contribute toward the support of the missionary, they are more likely to pray for the missionaries and to feel that the mission belongs to them. The Friends Missionary Prayer Band in south India is supported by more than 600 prayer groups, whose members give sacrificially and meet regularly for intercessory prayer. As for missionary preparation, the indigenous societies are convinced that it is better to train their missionaries in the local cultural context than to send them off to the West for schooling in a foreign setting. It is true that many of the instructors in these training centers have received their degrees in mission and evangelism in Western seminaries, but they have adapted the basic principles and methods to their own situations. The emphasis is not on academics and degrees, but on practical training and experience.

Another interesting feature is that the Third World societies are strongly biblical and evangelical in their theology. Belief in the authority of God's Word, in the sinfulness of humankind, and in Christ as the only Saviour has motivated Third World churches to become involved in missions and to organize mission societies. Most missionaries sent out are engaged in evangelism and church planting, but they are also significantly involved in social concerns. Eastern churches reject the division of human beings into various compartments—soul, mind, and body—and refuse to take part in the evangelism-versus-social action debate. They look upon the person as a unit and seek to minister to all human needs. Their missionaries proclaim that Christ not only saves from sin, but also helps reap a good crop, heals the sick, defeats demonic forces, and delivers from individual guilt.

Advantages of Third World Missions

Third World missions have certain advantages over Western missions. Because of past history, Western missionaries have often been identified with colonialism and imperialism. Afro-Asian missionaries are free from such ties. There is also a certain cultural similarity between people of one Eastern country and another. It is easier for missionaries to identify with the people whom they are serving. For these reasons, Third World missionaries—and thus their message—are more readily accepted than their Western counterparts.

Then again, there is the financial advantage. It costs far less to support a non-Western missionary. The average annual cost for a North American missionary is almost $22,000, while in India it is about $1,000. In Brazil, where approximately 746 national missionaries serve in both foreign and domestic endeavors, missionaries receive between $6,000 and $9,000 yearly. Non-Western missionaries are accustomed to a more simple lifestyle and find it easier to live on the level of the people.

In the third place, Third World mission societies are not bound to follow Western organizational structures. Some seem to be involved in mission with little or no structures;

others possess a simplified structure to complete one particular mission (like the Aymara Indian to the Navaho Indian). Western missions have often been guilty of having top-heavy organizations and imposing their structures on the younger churches. Third World missions are able to avoid this mistake.

Perhaps the greatest difference between Western missions and Third World missions is found in the vantage point. Because of higher national economies on the home front, Western missions have entered the Afro-Asian and Latin American countries from a position of strength, with more money and bigger organizations. But this has turned out to be a source of weakness rather than strength. We have overwhelmed the mission field with our abundance and made Christians dependent upon us. We have built schools and hospitals for them and given them free education and medical treatment. We have built churches and paid pastors' salaries. All this has stifled the initiative and spiritual growth of the national Christians. That they have now grown up and thrown off the shackles is a real cause for rejoicing.

On the other hand, Third World missions proceed from a position of seeming weakness, with little money and simple organizational structures. But this is turning out to be a real source of strength. They don't have much money to dole out; they are unable to construct large buildings. They can, however, make a spiritual impact. New converts should therefore learn to stand on their own feet and grow up much faster. This is a very significant advantage.

We must not get the impression, however, that everything is easy for Third World missions. Their missionaries are running into the same problems that Western missionaries have to face. They too find it difficult to learn strange languages, are prone to discouragement and loneliness, wonder how they will educate their children in a foreign culture, and face opposition and closed doors. We in the West need to pray just as hard for the Afro-Asian missionaries as we do for our own.

Neither must we get the impression that Third World missionaries want to go it all alone. They desire to establish their own societies and make their own decisions, but they are anxious for cooperation with Western churches. These are days for true partnership in world missions. The task of reaching the entire world for Christ is so staggering that no single church on earth can do the job. It will take the combined resources in finances and personnel of Christian churches in all countries to meet the challenge. We have already mentioned how Mission Aviation Fellowship, a Western-based organization, is flying Dyak missionaries from one part of Kalimantan to another, to carry the Gospel to neighboring tribes that are isolated by mountains and rivers. In June 1965, the century-old China Inland Mission reorganized to become the Overseas Missionary Fellowship, with headquarters in Singapore. This society recruits Western and Asian missionaries of many nationalities to carry out its mission in Asia. Korean churches and World Vision (based in Monrovia, California) formed a partnership in 1980 to assist Indonesian churches in planting 100 new congregations over a two-year period. They achieved their objective and have now set new goals.

New Chapters in Mission History
Third World missionaries are returning from their fields these days with remarkable stories of how the Holy Spirit is working in situations and in people's lives. They are helping to write new chapters in the Book of Acts. Many miracles are taking place through the Spirit's power. The sick are being healed (including those bitten by poisonous cobras), evil spirits are being cast out, missionaries are being delivered from danger, and above all, lives are being wonderfully transformed. Only a few of these stories can be told here, but they are examples of how God is manifesting His power all across the world today.

God's silent guards. Two south Indian women missionaries were going through a forest in north India, on their way to deliver food and money to a small mission center. Unaware that they were being stalked by a band of robbers, they were conversing on God's goodness and blessings. Coming upon an abandoned hut beside the path, they realized how tired they were and decided to stop for a rest. They lay down on the sagging porch and were soon sound asleep.

Their stalkers squatted down in the jungle grass, waiting until the women were asleep. Then their leader began creeping very slowly toward the hut. He was careful not to make any noise. His head bobbed up above the foliage, and he motioned for the others to follow him. Crouching over, they approached the porch. Suddenly the leader stopped them cold—he seemed to be in shock. They all stood up to look and stared with their mouths open—then suddenly turned and fled. The women slept on, undisturbed.

Some weeks later a man came to the women's house to meet them. No doubt he had known for some time where they lived. After greeting them he confessed to the two women that he was head of an outlaw band, and that they had intended to rob the women the day they had slept on a porch in the jungle. To their surprise, he asked them, "Who were the men standing guard over you as you were sleeping on the porch of that house?"

The two women shook their heads. "There were no men with us; we were alone. We had walked all day alone through the jungle."

The bandit insisted, "Oh no, you were not alone! All my men can tell you. We counted seventeen armed men standing guard over you while you slept! Of course we were afraid, and we ran away."

The women looked at each other and nodded their heads. "That's what God does!"

Later they wrote to their prayer group in south India and related how God had delivered them from the gang of thieves. By return mail they discovered the secret. At the very time the missionaries were in danger, their prayer group had met and was interceding for them. And that day the prayer group consisted of *exactly* seventeen men.

The book and the tiger. Rattan Boy was a policeman at Wagai, in the tribal area of southern Gujerat in India. He was a heavy drinker and came home drunk almost every night and usually beat his wife and children. They were all terrified of him. But one evening when the children came into the house, they discovered everything strangely quiet and peaceful. They asked their mother, "Where's Dad? Hasn't he come home yet?"

"Yes," answered their mother, "he's home. He's reading the Book."

"Why isn't he shouting and beating us like he usually does?"

The mother again replied, "He's in the next room reading the Book. It's the Book! It seems to have made a change in his life."

The children's eyes opened wide—they were not able to believe this good fortune. A *book* could do this?

What happened was that one of the Indian missionaries had given Rattan Boy a copy of the New Testament. As he read it, the Spirit of God began to get hold of his mind and heart. Then he cried out, "Oh, Jesus, You healed so many sick people and delivered others from evil spirits. Surely You can do something for an old drunk like me!" As a result, Jesus came into his heart and he was gloriously converted.

The news spread quickly through the village: "Rattan Boy is a changed man! And it's all on account of the Book! It's the Book!"

One evening not long afterward when Rattan Boy came home from work, a mother came carrying her sick child and laid him at his feet. "Sir," she said, "your God seems to be all-powerful. He has changed your life. Can He deliver my child from this terrible fever? He is already in a coma."

"Yes, He can," replied Rattan Boy. So saying he knelt down before the child and asked the Lord to heal him. Immediately the boy opened his eyes and smiled. From then on, every evening when Rattan Boy came home from work, he was besieged with sick and needy people, pleading for his prayers of healing. The Lord gave him this wonderful gift and many were healed through his ministry.

All these healings made the local witch doctor very angry. Formerly, the sick used to come to *his* door for help, and this was a good source of income for him. Now because of Rattan Boy, he had lost his crowd and his money. So he shouted out in rage in the village, "I am going to call on the gods and goddesses and on all the evil spirits to destroy this Rattan Boy!"

A few days later, word went through the village—"Everyone beware! There is a man-eating tiger in the area. Already he has killed and eaten three people! Don't sleep outside at night! Don't go deep into the jungle! Beware!"

But one night it was oppressively hot, and Rattan Boy said to his wife and children, "Let's sleep outside on our porch tonight. It's too hot in the house."

His wife warned him of the man-eating tiger, but he replied, "Don't be afraid. God will protect us."

God did. The next morning they could see the pug marks of the tiger. It had come down past the long row of houses in the village. Evidently, it stopped a short distance in front of Rattan Boy's house and sat on its haunches, observing the family asleep on the porch. But then it turned and went on down the row of houses, to the very last house where the witch doctor and his family lived.

Early in the morning the witch doctor's fifteen-year-old daughter got up and went out into the bushes for her toilet. The tiger jumped on her, seized her by the neck, and carried her off into the jungle. When it was daylight, they found the mangled remains of her body.

Then the people of the village said, "Look, Rattan Boy's family slept outside but they were not harmed. The witch doctor and his family slept inside, but the tiger killed and ate the daughter. Rattan Boy's God is greater than the gods of the witch doctor!" As a result, practically the whole village came to faith in Christ, including the witch doctor himself!

A siren and an earthquake. At a coal mine in the interior of China, it was the job of a young Chinese girl to blow the siren at 5:00 in the evening as a signal to the miners that their day's work was done. She and her family were Christians who worshiped secretly in a house church. One day about 1:30 in the afternoon, the girl heard an inner voice saying, "Go, blow the siren!"

That's a stupid idea, she thought. *I'm supposed to blow the siren at 5:00 P.M. If I blow it at 1:30 what will they do to me? They'll put me in jail for sure!*

But the inner voice was insistent, "Go, blow the siren." So in fear and trembling, she set off the siren. The miners were puzzled, but fearing it was some sort of warning, they started pouring out of the mine. Shortly after they were all out, an earthquake shook the area, destroying tunnels and blocking entrances to the mine.

In astonishment the miners huddled around the young girl and asked, "Why did you blow the siren way ahead of time? If we had been down there in the mine, we would have all been killed. What made you do it?"

The girl answered, "It was Jesus whom I worship who ordered me to blow the siren."

"Who is this Jesus?" they asked with one voice.

"Let me call my mother," said the girl. "She will be able to tell you better than I can."

The mother was a mature and committed Christian, and as the miners listened closely, she took thirty or forty minutes to tell them the Good News of Jesus. When she finished and gave an invitation, many of those hardened miners who had been brought up in atheism knelt then and there and receivedceived Christ as Saviour.

Yes, the Spirit of God is writing new chapters in the Book of Acts every day!

PART SIX

NEW OPEN DOORS—What Is God Doing?

While many doors across the seas are closing to foreign missions, a new evangelistic opportunity has opened right on our doorstep. In recent years an increasing flow of Asian and Latin American immigrants have entered our country. Asians are non-Christian by religion: Muslims, Hindus, and Buddhists. The American church needs to be aware of the situation and make an all-out effort to win these ethnic minorities to Christ and the church. Latin Americans are nominal Catholics, untouched by the church, and need to be led into a personal experience with Christ.

All is not lost for foreign missions either. New doors for service and witness are opening for laypersons in places where professional missionaries cannot go. Evangelical Christians in America need to seize these opportunities to be ambassadors for Christ in difficult yet needy areas of the world.

FIFTEEN

MISSIONS ON OUR DOORSTEP

The field is the world."

These words of Jesus found in Matthew 13:38 are very pertinent to our present world situation. The entire geographical world has reverted to a mission field. Formerly, we used to divide the world into two distinct camps—the Christian West and the non-Christian East. This appeared to be a neat and simple division, since the Christian faith was confined largely to Europe and the Americas, while the great world religions, such as Islam, Hinduism, Buddhism, and animism, held sway in Asia and Africa. But now the church of Jesus Christ is established, at least to some extent, in every part of Afro-Asia, and Christians are found all across the world. At the same time, Christianity has suffered major setbacks in Western countries, and some are even talking of a post-Christian era in Europe and the United States. It is quite evident that there are no real Christian nations anywhere in the world, but there are genuine followers of Christ in almost every land.

On the one hand, the home churches of the West do not hold an uncontested position in their own culture. Many persons have no connection with, and no respect for, the Christian church. They do not accept the norms of Christian behavior as their pattern for living. On the other hand, the mission-founded churches of the East are set in societies strongly influenced, or even controlled, by non-Christian religions. This means that every Christian congregation, regardless of location, is in an environment that is definitely missionary in character. The frontier between Christian and non-Christian is therefore not geographical, but spiritual. The line of demarcation is that of faith and unfaith. The mission field is not simply "over there" or "across the seas" but is everywhere and at our doorstep.

For the past few centuries the world missionary movement has been in one direction—from west to east. Christians from Europe and North America have been sending their messengers to the countries of Africa and Asia. But in recent years the movement has begun to flow in the opposite direction as well—from east to west. So we hear of the Hare Krishna movement, Zen Buddhism, Black Muslims, Bahaism, Transcendental Meditation, and Yoga right here in the United States. Hindu temples and Muslim mosques have been and are being built in many of our major cities. Thousands of our young people have been "converted" to these various religious movements in the past two decades; the United States is fast becoming a pluralistic religious society. Options in the field of religion are becoming more numerous.

This means the confrontation between religions is no longer confined to the Eastern countries. It is now all around us. No longer are Christians only in India and Pakistan and Sri Lanka rubbing shoulders with Hindus, Muslims, and Buddhists. Christians in England and Canada and the United States are regularly meeting followers of Krishna and Mohammed and Buddha. Today in England, the birthplace of Methodism, there are more Muslims than there are Methodists.

Unevangelized Areas in the United States
Americans probably have more opportunity to hear the Gospel than any other nation. Consider our advantages:
- There are nearly 490,000 clergy in the United States.
- There are 343,000 churches.
- Evangelicals own and operate 1,400 Christian radio stations (1 out of 6 in the U.S.). There are two Christian TV networks using earth satellite stations and beaming live programs 24 hours daily. Besides, there are Christian programs

on hundreds of local stations. All in all, Americans are exposed to nearly 2 million religious programs annually, aired over some 7,000 radio and TV stations.
• Two thousand new religious books are published annually. Bibles are everywhere; there is one in every hotel room.
The fact is, however, that America is not nearly as evangelized as it may first appear. Consider these significant statistics:
• Forty percent of the population is not connected with any church. In Alaska the figure is 90 percent; in Hawaii, 70 percent. This constitutes 94 million people.
• Only 38 percent of all Protestants attend church regularly, i.e., 26.6 million out of 70 million. This means a large majority of Protestant church members need to be reached for Christ. Statistics for the Roman Catholic Church are equally alarming.
• According to George Gallup, the evangelical community (those who claim a personal experience with Christ) includes only 45 million, less than 20 percent of the populace. This makes the United States one of the largest mission fields in the world with approximately 90 million to be evangelized.
• Among the unevangelized groups in the United States are 27 million cultists, 10 million alcoholics, 6 million Jews, 4 million who pass through the penal system each year, 3 million Muslims, and 1.4 million native Americans.
Black Americans in 1984 numbered 28 million, 12 percent of the populace. Only four countries of black Africa have a greater population than black America. Earl Parvin in *Missions U.S.A.* reminds us that "black Americans are only 30% evangelized, whereas black Africans are 50% evangelized." Many blacks in the United States are turning to the cults, while 200,000 have turned to the Black Muslim movement.
The American Indian population (1.4 million) is a mission field; only 43 percent of the community consider themselves Christians. About half the Indian population live on or around nearly 100 reservations under the jurisdiction of the Bureau of Indian Affairs; the other half are scattered among major cities. The community has been resistant to the Gospel in the past because of the white people's insensitivity to

Indian culture and their shameful treatment of the Indians. Native Americans thought they had to accept the white culture to be Christians and found it difficult to accept the Gospel message from the lips of those whose word was seldom trustworthy in other areas.

Six million Jews in America are a mission field. They are overwhelmingly an urban people, with more than half of their number living in seven major cities. The largest Jewish city in the world is New York, which is home for 1,118,000 Jews. As a people they reject Jesus Christ as the Son of God, the Messiah, and resent attempts to convert them to the Christian faith. The church is partly to blame for this attitude because of its historical prejudice against the Jewish people and its insistence on making Gentiles out of Jewish converts. Moishe Rosen, founder of the Jews for Jesus (1973), initiated a new approach to Jews whereby they can believe in Christ as the Messiah and still maintain their Jewish culture and gather in Messianic Jewish congregations. From all indications, the Jew is more responsive to the Gospel now than ever before. One study reveals that between 18,000 to 33,000 Jews have been converted to Christianity since 1965. Jewish evangelism must now also include concern for thousands of Russian Jews who have immigrated to our shores in recent years and continue to come at the rate of 8,000 each year.

Hispanics, numbering approximately 25 million, constitute a large mission field within our borders. The United States has the fifth largest Spanish-speaking community in the world. There are more Hispanics living here than in all Central America or most South American countries. They are now the second largest ethnic minority after the blacks, but because of a higher birth rate they will soon become the largest. The state of California is 25 percent Hispanic and Texas is 20 percent. These two states are home for half of the Spanish-speaking populace living in the United States.

Hispanics are a mixed people, comprised of many ethnic groups, having come to the United States over a long period of time. In recent years most of them have come from Cuba, Central America, and Mexico. Cubans have been fleeing Fidel Castro's Marxist regime; El Salvadorans are fleeing a difficult political situation in Central America. Mexicans, seeking jobs and a better way of life, constitute 60 percent of the Hispanics in the United States today. It is estimated that there are several million Mexicans in this country who have slipped across the border illegally. Many are migrants, with no skills or knowledge of English, moving about with the fruit and vegetable crops.

Hispanics are for the most part an urban people. The largest concentration is in Los Angeles, where 2 million Hispanics have created the fourth largest Mexican city in the world. New York City has the next largest community with 1.5 million, predominantly Puerto Ricans. Miami has 700,000 Cubans and is 40 percent Hispanic. Chicago has 580,000 Hispanics (unofficially 1 million). San Antonio's population is 54 percent Hispanic.

There are deep spiritual needs among Hispanic people in our midst. Back in their homelands they were Roman Catholic—in name at least—but when they arrived in this country they got lost to the church. Most Hispanics do not attend church because they were never made to feel welcome. They are a spiritually abused and neglected people.

Evangelicals need to be aware of the presence of Hispanics and concerned about their spiritual needs. We need to love these people and identify with their particular problems. The Pentecostal and Charismatic movements are especially attractive to Hispanics, for they appeal to their open, warm feelings and respond to their felt needs. Services are in Spanish, with nationals leading. Among mainline Protestant groups, Southern Baptists have been most successful in reaching the Spanish-speaking people. They have established 1,400 churches, most of which have Hispanic pastors, serving a Christian community of 150,000. The Assemblies of God, American Baptists, and Nazarenes have also done fairly well. Some churches have engaged Spanish-speaking evangelists to develop a Hispanic congregation that uses the same facilities as the Anglo church. Others have supported home mission organizations that have a burden to reach the Hispanics of the United States.

There is desperate need for a trained clergy among Hispanic congregations. Bible colleges and seminaries should make special provisions for scholarships and programs to train Hispanic evangelists and pastors to work among their people. A great harvest is right around the corner, if we will but seize the glorious opportunity that faces us.

The Asian Invasion

In the past two decades the mosaic of American society has become more colorful and complex than ever before. In the early years of American history, the greatest number of immigrants came from the British Isles—England, Scotland, Ireland, and Wales. Since their mother tongue was English, it was rather easy for them to be assimilated into American society and lose their original identity. Later came immigrants from Europe—Germany, France, Italy, Scandinavia, and so on—speaking a variety of languages and representing different cultural backgrounds. However, their languages had a common base and all used the Roman script, and their cultures came under the same European umbrella. It was more difficult for these people to be assimilated into the American system than for the British, but within a generation or two the process was more or less complete. American society was still considered a melting pot where a number of subcultures had come together in a new blend.

In the last twenty years, however, the picture has changed. The Immigration Act of 1965, signed by President Johnson, modified the system that had favored Europeans, opening up large-scale immigration from the Third World. The new rule put a ceiling of 20,000 from each country, but additional family members swelled the numbers. Thus, whereas the number of immigrants in the 1930s was 53,000 per year, by the 1980s it increased to 600,000 per year. And whereas in 1964 the number of Europeans was 54.8 percent of all immigrants, and that of Asians was only 5.1 percent, in 1984 it was 30.3 percent Asians and 22 percent Europeans. Refugees and their families are admitted as immigrants, and this adds to the flow. Since the close of the Vietnam War, approximately 510,000 refugees have been admitted from South Vietnam, Laos, and Kampuchea alone. The total number of bona fide immigrants that entered the United States in 1984 from all countries was 600,000. It is quite possible that an equal number of illegal immigrants brought the total to well over a million. These foreigners scatter across the 50 states, but California, Texas, and New York receive the lion's share. According to the 1984 statistics there were 14 million ethnics in addition to blacks, native Americans, and Hispanics within the United States.

Asian immigrants, numbering 5 million at present, have brought their languages, cultures, and religions with them. Chinese, Japanese, and Vietnamese have brought Buddhism; East Indians have brought Hinduism; and Arabs from the Middle East have brought Islam. These ethnic groups tend to live together in urban communities and are as unreached by the Gospel as they were back in their homelands. One of the large Muslim concentrations in the United States is in New York City and northern New Jersey, where 128,000 from twenty-five ethnic backgrounds live. In Detroit, Michigan's Arab Village, there are 100,000 Muslims; in Los Angeles, 200,000. There are at present 300 Islamic centers in 41 states across the country, including 84 mosques. A few mosques, such as the ones in Washington, D.C., Plainfield, Indiana; and Detroit, Michigan, are ornate structures costing millions of dollars. In the same manner, Hindus have brought their idols and worship patterns with them. In the Pittsburgh area, where several hundred Indian families have settled, a one-half-million-dollar shimmering white Hindu temple stands east of the city, near Monroeville. Numerous idols imported from India have been installed in the temple. Hindu priests, wearing native garments, perform their rituals in an Indian language. Two other Hindu temples have been constructed in the borough of Queens, New York City, for the convenience of several thousand Hindus in the area. In Flushing alone, an estimated 21,000 East Indians reside.

The following is a partial list of Asian and Middle East Americans in the United States at the present time:

Chinese—	1,000,000
Koreans—	1,000,000
Filipinos—	800,000
Japanese—	700,000
Indochinese—	510,000

Indians—	500,000
Thais—	120,000
Iranians—	200,000
Palestinians—	110,000

The Ethnic Challenge

These statistics show that the United States has become the most pluralistic ethnic and religious country on the face of the earth. We are becoming increasingly more diverse. People have gathered here from all nations, bringing their customs, beliefs, and lifestyles with them. As Peter Wagner has suggested, we are no longer a melting pot, but a stew pot, with all ingredients enriching each other, but each one seeking to maintain its own identity and uniqueness. Asian immigrants will not be assimilated into American society as quickly or as easily as Europeans. Even if they do become Americanized socially and culturally, they will still want to hold on to their religions. The "mission field" has been brought to our very doorstep. Non-Christian people have come to us from countries where Christian missionaries are not permitted to enter, such as Iraq, Iran, and Saudi Arabia. As Americans we are faced with one of the greatest missionary challenges of our history. While man has been closing the door to missionary service in many parts of the world, God has opened a new door right in our midst. We don't need to bother about visas and plane fare to reach these people; they are living all around us. And because of our free society, these people are more reachable and winnable here than they could possibly have been in their own tight-knit and closed societies in their homelands. They are free from many of the social and political pressures back home and can more readily choose to follow Christ in their newly adopted land.

The new situation has put the ordinary church member in the United States right on the front line of missions. No longer is it necessary to go to India to witness to a Hindu, to the Middle East to witness to a Muslim, or to Thailand to witness to a Buddhist. Followers of these religions are living all around us. We can witness to them in our own language.

Recently a committed Christian couple in Lexington, Kentucky met a young Hindu salesman from India in the course of their busines. They invited him to dinner one evening, and while seated around the table, they shared with him their personal faith in Jesus Christ. They found the young man very open to the Gospel, and before midnight this couple had the privilege of leading him into a personal experience with the Saviour. Not long afterward, I had the joy of baptizing the new convert into the Christian faith. More recently, this Christian couple has been able to lead the young man's sister, brother, and new bride to Christ. This all happened, not in far-off India, but right here in Kentucky!

It is a sad but true fact that few of our church members here in the homeland are prepared for this new confrontation, and thus they are unable to seize the evangelistic opportunities all about them. Since many are not fully committed to Christ themselves, they have nothing to offer people of other faiths. Others know little or nothing of these other religions and don't know how to witness intelligently to Hindus, Muslims, Buddhists, etc. Our pastors and churches will have to do a better job preparing our people spiritually and mentally for the missionary task confronting us.

The American church has a tremendous responsibility and opportunity to win the growing immigrant population for Christ. Regardless of how some may feel about "so many foreigners coming into our country and messing things up," these people are here to stay and they are on our hands. Are we going to ignore them and leave them to worship their idols and strange gods, or are we going to introduce them to the living God and a new life in Christ?

Some denominations are already doing a commendable work among the ethnic minorities. At the top of the list are the Southern Baptists. Their Language Missions Department, under the leadership of Dr. Oscar Romo, has set the pace over the last ten or fifteen years. Southern Baptists are the most ethnically diverse denomination, worshiping in 87 languages in more than 4,000 language-culture congregations every Sunday. This is an aggregate of 200,000 ethnic believers praising God in their own churches. Over 20,000 new ethnics in new congregations are professing faith in Jesus Christ each year through their ministry. Other denominations significantly crossing ethnic barriers in the United

States include the Church of the Nazarene and the Assemblies of God. The Christian and Missionary Alliance churches have assumed the Vietnamese refugees as their prime responsibility, for until recently Vietnam was one of their major mission fields. Missionaries who were forced out of Vietnam after the war are concentrating on working among these people. Many of these ethnic congregations worship in the same sanctuary as the Anglo congregation, but at different hours. In a few places, as many as four different language groups are worshiping in the same church on Sunday.

The Christian Church in Korea, a fast-growing and spiritually alive church, is doing an excellent job in following up Korean immigrants to the United States and winning them for Christ. Since 1970, 430 Korean churches have been planted by national pastors in the Los Angeles area alone. One pastor, Kwang Shin Kim, who had been a successful landscape architect, was converted in 1978 and decided to enter Talbot Seminary and plant a Christian and Missionary Alliance church in Norwalk, near Los Angeles. The church grew rapidly and leased an entire unused high school campus. They are already nearly filling the 2,000-seat auditorium on Sundays, and Pastor Kim's goal is to have 7,000 members by 1988. The church also has a missions program with an annual budget of almost .5 million dollars, and they hope to increase this to $2.5 million by 1988. They have already established Filipino and Cambodian congregations as well as an Anglo congregation. The Korean church pays the Anglo pastor's salary.

In April 1985, a National Convocation on Evangelizing Ethnic America was held in Houston, Texas for four days. The 683 registrants represented 63 ethnic groups and 47 denominations and organizations. This was an attempt to sensitize churches in the United States to the mission field on their doorstep and to make concrete plans to meet this challenge. In order to reach ethnic America for Christ, the Houston convocation emphasized taking the following four steps:

Awareness. Churches must become aware of the presence of ethnic groups in their midst. Urban churches in particular need to make a survey and discover who lives in their neighborhoods. Census material and the telephone directory can be a big help in this regard. Are there Koreans living in your community? East Indians? Vietnamese? Are there any Christians among them? Such individuals can be key contact persons and potential leaders.

Concern. Anglo congregations should be motivated to reach these people for Christ. Christians should be just as concerned about the lost at home as they are about those who are lost across the seas. We send missionaries to India to preach the Gospel; how about witnessing to Indians living in America? We would like to send missionaries to Arabs in the Middle East, but can't; how about trying to win Arabs living a few blocks away?

Prayer. We should motivate entire congregations to pray for the salvation of their non-Christian neighbors. We need to pray for guidance in strategy and for release of the power of the Holy Spirit.

Plan of action. Just putting up a sign and inviting ethnics to come to church will not bring results. We must go after them—make contact with them, make friends, seek to meet their special needs (giving instruction in English, for example), and witness to them. Perhaps we can start a home Bible study. If there are one or two Christians of the same ethnic background, let them take the lead. When an interested group emerges, we can provide church facilities for their meetings and allow them to worship, sing, and preach in their own language, in which they feel most at home. The hope is that a congregation will eventually be formed with its own pastor and leaders. Then the new Christians will take the lead in winning the rest of their people for Christ.

A new and exciting challenge is facing America's churches. We darWe dare not, we must not fail. God grant us wisdom and grace to face this challenge courageously, for the upbuilding of God's kingdom and for His glory.

SIXTEEN

TENTMAKER MISSIONS

The day of the lay missionary has dawned! Unprecedented opportunities are opening up for Christians to be ambassadors for Christ while engaging in their professions abroad. Laypersons are beginning to realize that they have a strategic role to play in the church's worldwide mission. They don't have to be "professional missionaries," ordained by the church and supported by the mission, in order to be bearers of the Good News of Christ. They can be unofficial, self-supporting witnesses for Christ through their own secular jobs.

There is scriptural precedence for this type of lay witness. Dr. Christy Wilson, Jr., professor of Missions and Evangelism at Gordon-Conwell Theological Seminary, reminds us that many godly men and women in the Old Testament were self-supporting witnesses. Abraham was a cattle raiser, Hagar a domestic worker, Isaac a farmer, Rebekah a water carrier, Rachel a sheepherder, Joseph a premier, Miriam a baby-sitter, and Moses a flock grazer. Joshua was a military commander, Rahab an innkeeper, Samson a champion fighter, Ruth a gleaner, Boaz a grain grower, David a ruler, Asaph a composer, Solomon an emperor, the Queen of Sheba an administrator, Job a gentleman farmer, Amos a sharecropper, Daniel a prime minister, Queen Esther a ruler, and Nehemiah a governor.

In the New Testament also we find that many key characters were laypersons. Joseph, our Lord's stepfather, was a carpenter, Martha was a housekeeper, Zaccheus a tax collector, Nicodemus and Joseph of Arimathea were supreme-court councilors, Barnabas was a landowner, Cornelius a Roman officer, Luke a doctor. Priscilla, Aquila, and Paul were tentmakers, Lydia was a seller of cloth, Zenas a lawyer, and Erastus a city treasurer. In the early church it was lay Christians who, because of the persecution, "went everywhere preaching the Word" (J. Christy Wilson, Jr., *Today's Tentmakers,* Tyndale House Publishers, pp. 20–21).

The Apostle Paul was the finest model of a self-supporting missionary. He was a tentmaker by trade and used his skill as a means of paying his expenses on his missionary journeys. It was while making tents with Aquila and Priscilla that he led them to Christ. For this reason the lay witness of today is often referred to as a tentmaking missionary. A tentmaker is any dedicated Christian who lives and works overseas and who uses his secular calling as an opportunity to give his personal witness to Jesus Christ.

Tentmakers on Tour

Opportunities for tentmaker witnessing are varied. Many laypersons, instead of taking a vacation on a beach somewhere and lying idly in the sun, are joining Christian work teams and taking a "vacation with God" on some mission field, for a period of ten to fourteen days out of the year. A growing number of churches and organizations are coordinating such work tours.

In 1969, Rev. Maurice Stevens, a United Methodist evangelist in the Kentucky conference, established Missionary World Service and Evangelism, Inc., a not-for-profit organization with offices in Wilmore, Kentucky. Leaders of this agency conduct several work tours each year, taking groups of laypersons to such countries as India, Kenya, Costa Rica and Honduras, Colombia, Finland, and Arizona and New Mexico here in the United States to help American Indian missions. Team members pay their own way or are sent by their churches. The group usually consists of masons, carpenters, plumbers, and electricians, who during their stay will help build a chapel, a classroom, or some other building needed on a particular mission station. During daylight hours they work hard on construction, and then in the evenings they hold religious services and give their personal testimonies. Because of their willingness to "get down in the dirt" and work side by side with nationals, these team members and their witness are well received by the people, and many come to Christ as a result.

In response to a growing grassroots movement in missions, the Southeastern Jurisdiction of the United Methodist Church in 1976 established a coordinating office in Atlanta, directed by Rev. Thomas L. Curtis. Known as the United Methodist Volunteers in Mission (UMVIM), the agency serves 17 annual conferences in nine different states. In 1984, over 1,400 volunteers participated in church-related projects overseas, financed by almost 1 million dollars in contributions. Some 2,500 to 3,000 volunteers from the jurisdiction worked on similar projects in the United States.

Thousands of young people are involved each summer in work and witness teams both at home and abroad. In the summer of 1984, approximately 4,000 teenage volunteers from across the country repaired homes and built six houses for the needy in a four-state area in Appalachia. The work was coordinated by the Appalachia Service Project. In 1985, Youth with a Mission (YWAM) sent out 5,000 young people all across the world to distribute Christian literature and engage in person-to-person witnessing. At the same time, 4,000 young people went out under the direction of an organization called Operation Mobilization.

Various reasons are given for the appeal of the volunteer mission movement: the exciting, life-changing experience of personal involvement and personal relationships; hands-on way to express faith; the spontaneity of the program that comes from the people and not from a committee. One thing is for sure: people who go on these work teams come back excited about missions. For the first time, missions are not something far-off that they hear about secondhand from some missionary home on furlough but something personal and close at hand that they have seen for themselves. For years these church members thought that missions were carried out only by seminary-trained professional personnel;

now they see that a carpenter, a mechanic, a homemaker, or a student can get involved, if only for a brief period. They in turn, through their enthusiasm, influence other members of their congregations to become interested and involved in missions.

Christian medical personnel—surgeons, dentists, ophthalmologists, and nurses—have a special opportunity for tentmaking ministries abroad. On many mission fields church-operated hospitals are suffering from a severe shortage of staff and are crying out for help. They are deeply appreciative of physicians who come to the field and give them a lift for a month or two in specialized service. In some cases, such as remote mountain sections in Mexico, there are no medical facilities whatsoever. Teams of Christian doctors, representing various fields of medicine, have found great joy and personal satisfaction in setting up ten-day or two-week clinics and ministering to poverty-stricken people, free of charge, in such needy places. Through their loving service these medical persons have introduced many patients to the redeeming love of Christ.

When the Belgian Congo (now Zaire) in Africa received its independence from Belgium several years ago, the departure of thousands of Europeans left a leadership vacuum that has taken a long time to fill. The exodus of more than 500 doctors made a serious public health situation even more dangerous. Thousands of Zairians, emaciated with malnutrition and stricken with an assortment of rare jungle diseases, threw themselves on the mercy of a handful of mission hospitals and already overworked doctors. In response to that emergency, Bishop Richard C. Raines of the Methodist Church summoned 55 doctors in Indianapolis, Indiana to a special breakfast, explained the situation to them, and challenged volunteers to leave their practices for three months to serve mission hospitals in Zaire. He said their travel expenses would be paid, but other costs must be borne by the doctors themselves. At that meeting 6 physicians offered their services and later 4 others volunteered.

Doctors Richard M. Nay, heart specialist, and James M. Jay, internal medicine expert, were typical of the entire group. They returned home with a missionary zeal that would fire the heart of even the most doubtful skeptic. Their speaking schedule for the first few months following their return left district missionary secretaries gasping. Dr. Nay, speaking an average of three times a week from one end of the state to the other, appeared before more than 100,000 people within four months. Among his most attentive audiences were city and county medical societies, directors of metropolitan banks, and service clubs. He held 600 students entranced at a high school convocation and drew the greatest crowd in history for a missions meeting at a large suburban Presbyterian church.

Dr. Nay, in explaining the transformation that took place in his own life, gave the following testimony: "Before I went to Zaire I had more or less ignored the cause of missions. When missionaries came to speak at my church, I seldom went because I was so busy. But after months of exposure to overwhelming needs of the Zaire people and what the church is doing to meet them, I am convinced missions is the most effective and important force for good in the world today. The memories are indelible. I can't help but eat, sleep, and drink missions after this experience."

Dr. Jay, who served at a mission hospital in Kimpese in Central Zaire, had this to say about his experience: "We Americans simply cannot picture the primitive conditions in which our mission doctors work. I recall one time when we interrupted surgery to chase a goat out of the operating room. And on one occasion we found cats sleeping in the beds of the maternity ward!"

Tentmakers Serving Abroad

An even more significant open door for the tentmaker witness is that of residing and working abroad in some secular job and using that opportunity to be an ambassador for Christ. In a number of areas in the world, career missionaries are not permitted to enter, but people with specialized skills are welcomed by the government. This is true of several countries in the Middle East. In each case a very orthodox form of Islam prevails, and Christian missionary activity is prohibited. But thousands of American technicians are working in the oil fields in these countries. No doubt a good number of committed Christians could be found in this group. If they could be trained and persuaded to be effective witnesses for Jesus Christ, they would add a whole new dimension to missionary endeavor.

The U.S. State Department claims that over 4 million Americans reside abroad. This means that for every Protestant missionary going out from North America, almost 100 other North Americans are living and working abroad. Even if only one-fourth of this number were regenerated persons, this would constitute a possible force of 1 million witnesses for Christ. The Southern Baptist Convention's foreign mission board estimates that perhaps 100,000 of their church members live abroad. The spiritual potential here is tremendous.

What happened in Afghanistan several years ago is a good illustration of what tentmaker witnessing can achieve for the cause of Christ. Afghanistan is a fanatical Muslim country and has never allowed Christian missionaries to enter. But in the early 1950s, just when the country was opening up to the outside world, a small group of committed Christians went from the United States to teach in Habibia College. Dick Soderberg led the group. He had been an instructor in engineering at the University of Southern California. He quickly saw that a top-notch technical school was needed in Afghanistan and drew up a proposal, which he presented to the Ministry of Education. The government accepted Soderberg's proposal, and Dick was appointed director of the new school and assigned to return to the United States to recruit a faculty and secure a library and equipment. The Afghan government agreed to give land for the new campus, as well as put up necessary buildings. Dick Soderberg lined up all necessary teachers and received contributions of thousands of dollars worth of texts and equipment for this new institute. Faculty members were all evangelical Christians, well qualified in their respective fields. For a number of years, these persons acted as a Christian presence in a staunch Muslim environment and witnessed for Christ to students and colleagues both by their lives and conversation. Evangelical Christians serving in U.S. Aid, Medico, and Peace Corps programs added their influence to this witness movement for Christ in Afghanistan. Sad to say, that door is now closed.

Nepal affords another classic illustration of great potential for tentmaking missions. For decades Nepal, a landlocked country, had been closed to the outside world and to Christian missions. Then God opened the door in a most unusual way.

Robert Fleming and his wife were Methodist missionaries teaching in a mission school in North India. Mr. Fleming was a bird-watcher by hobby and was an expert at it. In 1949 the Chicago Natural History Museum and the *National Geographic* magazine requested that he go to Nepal and get pictures and specimens of hundreds of beautiful birds that inhabit the Himalayan foothills. Fleming made two such trips into Nepal, accompanied by three missionary doctors (one of them his wife), who rendered invaluable medical service to the people while he was collecting birds. Good reports of these services reached the attention of the Nepalese government, and this led to an official invitation in 1953 to start medical work in Kathmandu, the capital, and Tansen. As a result, the United Mission to Nepal was established, with ten mission boards cooperating. Later the number of societies increased to twenty-three, representing ten different Protestant denominations, and lay missionaries came from India, Japan, Australia, the United Kingdom, and North America. Educational and agricultural work were added to the medical services with centers in a dozen places throughout Nepal.

According to the constitution of Nepal, no citizen may change religion. Each person must be brought up in the religion of his or her parents. So the United Mission was restricted to secular services, with no evangelism permitted. It was strictly a lay mission. Workers did find opportunities, however, to witness privately to patients and students. But God raised up Indian and Nepali evangelists to be in the front line of evangelistic endeavors and to lay the foundation for the church in Nepal.

Prem Pradhan, a Nepali Gurkha soldier who had served in the British army for fifteen years and was converted while in India, returned to his homeland in 1953, and started witnessing to his own people. When he baptized his first nine converts, he was arrested and put in prison for five years, and his converts were put in prison for one year. But he kept witnessing to the prisoners and won more converts in jail than out of jail.

Kunjukutti Athial from the Mar Thoma Syrian Church in South India was one of the first Indian evangelists to enter Nepal. Within a few years he had gathered a congregation in Kathmandu and built the first Christian church in the country. Today it is estimated that there are between ten and fifteen thousand Christians in Nepal. Many have spent time in jail or have been heavily fined, but they continue to take their stand for Christ.

How did it all start? With a Christian teacher going to Nepal to study birds!

Today a new door has opened for tentmaker witnesses in China, which has been closed to Christian missions for over thirty-five years. Now that China has opened up to the outside world for trade, its government is anxious for many of its citizens to study English, which they realize is fast becoming the international trade language. So the Chinese government is inviting hundreds of teachers from the West to come and teach English as a second language in colleges and universities. Many evangelical Christians in the States are seizing this opportunity to become a Christian presence and witness in a land that is probably one of the most spiritually hungry in the world today.

Mr. Welch (not his real name) is a highly successful attorney with his own law firm, doing millions of dollars worth of business each year. Both he and his wife are dedicated Christians and for years have been engaged in an effective lay ministry to hundreds of people in their hometown. But a few years ago they felt God calling them to be witnesses in mainland China. For a whole year they took lessons in the Mandarin language and studied as much as they could about China and its people. Then they sent in their résumés to the Chinese government, offering to teach in a university. In order to maintain complete honesty in their dealings with the government, the Welches stated very clearly: "While we make application to teach in a Chinese university, our purpose in coming to China is to tell the people about the saving grace of Jesus Christ, and the relationship with God which is available through Him." That they were accepted on these terms is proof of God's calling and intervention.

The Lord provided employment as professors at a Polytechnical University in the heart of China. Mrs. Welch was to teach English as a second language to students planning to come to America for study; Mr. Welch was to teach international law to "head workers" at factories and companies that do business with the United States. It was their plan that the classes they taught would open doors for ministry.

The Welches are having an exciting time in their new assignment. Mrs. Welch developed the idea of a "journal," a weekly one-page essay that students are required to write on any subject they choose. In turn she reads the journals and makes comments on them. It is an excellent way for students to practice their English, but also provides a way for them to express their deepest feelings and longings. With the passing of time these essays have become more and more personal, opening a way for Mrs. Welch to counsel with and witness to the students.

The Welches have also developed an open door policy in their home. Their apartment is always home to anyone, anytime, for language practice, counseling, socializing, and ministry. Students first come to "practice English" (or so they say), but then they start bringing up personal or spiritual matters that eventually lead to a discussion of God and His Son, Jesus Christ. Sometime later they come privately on an individual basis. Combining tact with love, the Welches have been able to lead several of the students into personal relationships with Christ. Students in turn start witnessing to and winning their roommates and family members.

Another committed layperson from the United States is serving as English professor in a strategic university in Tibet. He is the son of former missionaries to China and speaks Mandarin fluently. In a vast area where the Gospel has never penetrated, he acts as a solitary light in spiritual darkness. He has to be extremely careful of his contacts and conversations, but he believes that he is plowing ground and sowing seed for a future harvest. He sincerely believes that there will be a strategic breakthrough in Tibet through the mysterious working of the Holy Spirit within the next few years.

A missionary who serves in Hong Kong and has made several trips into China told me that Chinese officials have openly declared that they appreciate and prefer *Christian* teachers who have come into their country over secular-minded teachers. They can see a difference in Christian character and lifestyle!

These are but a few illustrations of dedicated laymen and laywomen, representing numerous denominations and a variety of occupations, who are becoming more and more personally involved in the worldwide missionary enterprise of the church. Carpenters, bricklayers, electricians, radio and television technicians, accountants, pharmicists, teachers, engineers—people in all walks of life—are beginning to understand something about missions. They see that missions is not the prerogative of the professional missionary or seminary graduate but is the responsibility and privilege of every Christian disciple. They are beginning to discover that missions is not a drab, dreary activity for colorless individuals suffering from a martyr complex, but an exciting, challenging, meaningful adventure for those who will deny themselves and lose themselves in service for Christ and humanity. Tity. They see that Christian missions is more than just a Peace Corps program directed from Washington. It is a Prince-of-Peace Corps movement directed by the Lord of the universe.

A CLOSING
CHALLENGE

In his first letter to the church at Corinth, the Apostle Paul wrote these words: "A wide door for effective work has opened to me, and there are many adversaries" (1 Cor. 16:9).

Here we have the perennial paradox of Christian missions: God opening a door, men and women trying to close it. On the one hand, opportunity; on the other, opposition. On one side, advantages; on the other, adversaries.

But notice where Paul places the emphasis. He did not major on the opposition, the adversaries. He could very easily have done so, for he had problems wherever he went. He was beaten, thrown into prison, ordered out of cities, shipwrecked. In spite of all this, he placed primary emphasis on the opportunities and just casually mentioned the adversaries. He gazed at the open door, and glanced at the opposition.

Today, in many Christian circles, we have reversed the order of emphasis. We keep talking about problems, the opposition: spirit of nationalism, specter of Communism, anti-Western criticism, "Yankee-go-home" attitude, closed doors, rising cost of missionary support, and so on. We are gazing at problems and missing open doors. But since when has the church ever struck its flag in the face of opposition? Jesus never promised an easy road; He did promise the comfort of His presence and the power of His Spirit. We need to get our eyes back on the sovereign Lord and focus on the opportunities. Whenever the human hand closes a door, God opens another. So there will never be any unemployment in God's business. We will always have a job to perform.

Human need is still the same around the world. People are lost and need a Redeemer. We need forgiveness and cleansing and power to live a victorious life. We need the dynamic of the Holy Spirit to fulfill God's plan for our lives. Some of us are hungry and need bread; some are poor and need a helping hand; others are victims of injustice and oppression and need deliverance and freedom. We need to be what God meant us to be.

The Gospel is still the power of God unto salvation to everyone who believes. There are many religions in the world, but only one Gospel. The world doesn't need more religion; it needs Christ. Religion can't save anyone, not even the Christian religion; Christ alone can save. In the Good News of Jesus Christ we have the answer to the sin-hurt of the world.

The Great Commission is still our marching orders and is binding on all Christians everywhere. We need to be obedient to the command of Christ and mobilize our total resources in finances and personnel for total evangelization of the world.

Jesus never commanded us to do anything that He wasn't willing to do Himself. There is not a single problem we face today that He did not face in His ministry on earth. He experienced misunderstanding, abuse and criticism, injustice, physical suffering, and even death. And He triumphed over all of these. So whenever you and I face any type of problem, we simply have to say to that particular problem, "Bend your neck." And sure enough, we see the footprints of the Son of God. He has already been that way and has triumphed completely. Thus, we do not strive *for* the victory; we work *from* the victory that Christ has already given us.

The Holy Spirit is working in strange and fantastic ways around the world today. He is working through non-Christian governments, adverse environmental factors, and all

kinds of people to open new doors for His people to proclaim the Good News of salvation and to build the church of
Jesus Christ around the world. We need to walk through
these doors while they are still open.

These are difficult yet challenging days. It is time for
advance, not retreat. Let us go forward in the power of the
Spirit to tell all people everywhere that God loves them,
Christ died for them, and they can be sons and daughters of
the King of kings. Let us be inexhaustible in this great harvest
of humanity!

BIBLIOGRAPHY

PART I

Braaten, Carl E. *The Flaming Center: A Theology of the Christian Mission.* Philadelphia: Fortress Press, 1977.

Glover, Robert H. *The Bible Basis of Missions.* Los Angeles: Bible House of Los Angeles, 1946.

Kane, J. Herbert. *Christian Missions in Biblical Perspective.* Grand Rapids, Mich.: Baker Book House, 1976.

Peters, George W. *A Biblical Theology of Missions.* Chicago: Moody Press, 1972.

Seamands, John T. *Around the World for Christ.* Berne, Ind.: Economy Press, 1973.

Trueblood, Elton. *The Validity of the Christian Mission.* New York: Harper and Row, 1972.

PART II

Armerding, Carl E. *Evangelicals and Liberation.* Nutley, N.J.: Presbyterian and Reformed Publishing Co., 1977.

Byerhaus, Peter. *Missions: Which Way?* Grand Rapids, Mich.: Zondervan, 1971.

Corbitt, Duvon C. *Liberation Theology.* Wilmore, Ky.: Asbury Press, 1981.

Glasser, Arthur F., and McGavran, Donald. *Contemporary Theologies of Mission.* Grand Rapids, Mich.: Baker Book House, 1983.

Gutierrez, Gustavo. *A Theology of Liberation.* Maryknoll, N.Y.: Orbis Books, 1973.

Hutcheson, Richard G., Jr. *Mainline Churches and the Evangelicals.* Atlanta: John Knox Press, 1981.

Kirk, J. Andrew. *Liberation Theology: An Evangelical View from the Third World.* Atlanta: John Knox Press, 1979.

McGavran, Donald, ed. *Crucial Issues in Missions Tomorrow.* Chicago: Moody Press, 1972.

Stott, John R.W. *Christian Mission in the Modern World.* Downers Grove, Ill.: InterVarsity Press, 1975.

Stott, John R.W. *The Lausanne Covenant.* Minneapolis, Minn.: World Wide Publications, 1975.

Recommended Articles for Part II
Asbury Seminarian, July 1977. Articles on liberation theology by Derek Winter and Joseph Wang.

Christianity Today, August 8, 1975. "The Theology of Liberation," by Rene Williamson.

Consultation on the Relationship between Evangelism and Social Action. Grand Rapids, Mich. Various published papers, 1982.

Eternity, July/August 1986. Articles on liberation theology by Ronald Nash, Ken Myers, and Dean Curry.

Good News, Summer 1974. "Evangelism and Social Action," by Stephen Mott.

PART III

Adeny, Miriam. *God's Foreign Policy.* Grand Rapids, Mich.: Eerdmans, 1984.

Fenton, Horace L. *Myths about Missions.* Downers Grove, Ill.: InterVarsity Press.

Greenway, Roger S. *Apostles to the City.* Grand Rapids, Mich.: Baker Book House, 1978.

Greenway, Roger S. *Discipling the City.* Grand Rapids, Mich.: Baker Book House, 1979.

Lacy, Creighton, ed. *Christianity amid Rising Men and Nations.* New York: Association Press, 1965.

Levai, Blaise. *Revolution in Missions.* Vellore, India: The Popular Press, 1957.

Manikam, Rajah B. *Christianity and the Asian Revolution.* New York: Friendship Press, 1954.

Seamands, John T. *Tell It Well.* Kansas City, Mo.: Beacon Hill Press, 1981.

Sider, Ronald J. *Rich Christians in an Age of Hunger.* Downers Grove, Ill.: InterVarsity Press, 1977.

Simon, Arthur. *Bread for the World.* Grand Rapids, Mich.: Eerdmans, 1975.

Sine, Tom. *The Mustard Seed Conspiracy.* Waco, Texas: Word Books, 1981.

World Relief. *State of the World in the 1980s.* Wheaton, Ill., 1980.

PART IV

Dodd, Carley H. *Dynamics of Intercultural Communication.* Dubuque, Iowa: William C. Brown Publishers, 1982.

Hesselgrave, David J. *Communicating Christ Cross-Culturally.* Grand Rapids, Mich.: Zondervan, 1978.

McGavran, Donald. *The Clash Between Christianity and Cultures.* Washington, D.C.: Canon Press, 1974.

Nida, Eugene A. *Customs and Cultures.* New York: Harper and Brothers, 1954.

Nida, Eugene A. *Message and Mission.* New York: Harper and Brothers, 1960.

Richardson, Don. *Peace Child.* Glendale, Calif.: Regal Books, 1974.

Richardson, Don. *Eternity in Their Hearts.* Ventura, Calif.: Regal Books, 1981.

Seamands, John T. *Tell It Well.* Kansas City, Mo.: Beacon Hill Press, 1981.

Stott, John R.W., ed. *Down to Earth: Studies in Christianity and Culture.* Grand Rapids, Mich.: Eerdmans, 1980.

PART V

Clark, Dennis E. *The Third World and Missions.* Waco, Texas: Word Books, 1971.

International Congress on World Evangelization, Lausanne, Switzerland. *Let the Earth Hear His Voice,* Papers and Responses. Minneapolis, Minn. World Wide Publications, 1975.

Keyes, Lawrence E. *The Last Age of Missions.* Pasadena, Calif.: William Carey Library, 1983.

McGavran, Donald. *The Bridges of God.* London: World Dominion Press, 1955.

McGavran, Donald. *How Churches Grow.* London: World Dominion Press, 1955.

McGavran, Donald. *Church Growth and Christian Mission.* New York: Harper and Row, 1965.

McGavran, Donald. *Understanding Church Growth.* Grand Rapids, Mich.: Eerdmans, 1980.

McGavran, Donald. *The Challenge of the Unreached Peoples.* Address given to the E.F.M.A. annual meeting, Colorado Springs, Colo., Sept. 27, 1982.

Nelson, Martin L. *The How and Why of Third World Missions.* Pasadena, Calif.: William Carey Library, 1976.

Nelson, Martin L., ed. *Readings in Third World Missions.* Pasadena, Calif.: William Carey Library, 1976.

Winter, Ralph and Hawthorne, Steven C., eds. *Perspectives on the World Christian Movement: A Reader.* Pasadena, Calif.: William Carey Library, 1981.

Winter, Ralph D. *Penetrating the Last Frontiers.* Pasadena, Calif.: William Carey Library, 1978.

Winter, Ralph D. *The Grounds for a New Thrust in World Mission.* Pasadena, Calif.: William Carey Library, 1977.

Wong, James; Larson, Peter; Pentecost, Edward. *Missions from the Third World.* Singapore: Church Growth Study Center, 1972.

Yamamori, Tetsunao, and Lawson, E. LeRoy. *Introducing Church Growth.* Cincinnati: Standard Publishing House, 1975.

Yamamori, Tetsunao, and Lawson, E. LeRoy. *Church Growth Is Everybody's Business.* Cincinnati: Standard Publishing House, 1975.

PART VI

Parvin, Earl. *Missions U.S.A.* Chicago: Moody Press, 1985.

Wilson, J. Christy, Jr. *Today's Tentmakers.* Wheaton, Ill.: Tyndale House Publishers, 1979.

Recommended Articles for Part VI

Time, July 8, 1985. "Immigrants: The Changing Face of America."

USA Today, June 30, 1986. Section E, devoted to immigrants.

Wagner, Peter. "A Vision for Evangelizing the Real America." Plenary session address given at the National Convocation on Evangelizing Ethnic America, Houston, Texas, April 15-19, 1985.

Walt, John D., Jr. "You Believe in God?" Paper submitted to Dr. J.T. Seamands, Asbury Theological Seminary, Wilmore, Ky., May 6, 1986.